CW01498303

ADVANCED RIDER TRAINER

THE HANDBOOK
FOR
TRAINING THE TRAINER

Advanced Rider Trainer
The Handbook for Training the Trainer

Publisher: Anixe Publishing Ltd England
Web: http://www.anixepublishing.co.uk
ISBN 978-0-9574523-3-6
First Edition January 2017
Copyright © 2017 Stephen Tucker and David Rainford

All Rights Reserved. No part of this publication may be reproduced, stored in a retrieval system, or transmitted in any form or by any means – by electronic, mechanical, photocopying, recording or otherwise – without prior written permission.

ACKNOWLEDGEMENTS

The authors would like to thank our wives for their love and understanding towards our second passion in life - motorcycling! In addition, a special thank you to Teresa and Carole, for proof reading so diligently for us.

We would also like to thank Bob Smalley for his kind words in the Foreword and all our biker friends for their encouragement and contributions.

Finally, our thanks to our publisher John Goodwin for making it happen.

FOREWORD

Advanced Rider Training has achieved what I believe it set out to do; that is to compliment Motorcycle Roadcraft. It provides a comprehensive insight into how, when, what and why to teach and learn the "ART" of motorcycle riding. The authors Steve and David have said it how it is based on their love of and lives spent riding bikes. Whether an experienced trainer or rider or just starting out this comprehensive handbook oozes knowledge and best practice; Give it a read; there is much to learn, and who knows, it may help you when you most need it.

BOB SMALLEY

Bob was formally Head of Motorway and Traffic Policing in the West Midlands and for 25 years Chief Examiner of RoSPA Advanced Drivers and Riders. He was a member of the Standing Advisory Board contributing to the content of the latest publication of Roadcraft and Motorcycle Roadcraft.

Table of Contents

PREFACE

There is no getting away from it, when the biking bug grabs hold of you, prepare to be well and truly hooked. Your bike gives you the freedom to get up and go whenever you want to. You and your bike become one. You are inseparable. You enjoy the thrills, your ride outs, the commute to work gets quicker and easier and the smile on your face gets bigger. You are having fun.

But with the thrills and enjoyment come the spills. Yes, being a biker means that you are more at risk of being killed or seriously injured than most other road users. Why? The majority of bikers who are killed or seriously injured took unnecessary risks or lacked the knowledge and skills to control their bike safely. Are the risks worth it? *The answer to that is a definite no!*

And to everyone associated with motorcycling, from manufacturers and dealers to insurance companies and clothing manufacturers, please realise the seriousness of this problem for you! Let us spell it out - *Dead customers do not provide repeat business*.

Insurance companies tell us that if you have had a crash you are three times more likely than the average person to have another. Why? It is really simple. Most people who have a crash blame it on something or somebody other than themselves. That means they do not need to change their own behaviour, so they don't. Then they have another crash...not an accident! You, the rider, are the one who must change if you are to survive. Not the bike, the bend, road surface or weather but the biker!

In fact, most crashes could have been avoided if riders had received some professional training. Riding a bike is a skill that has to be acquired. There are very few "natural riders" out there. Passing a national bike test has never adequately prepared riders for the hazards they face on the road. Unless and until major improvements are made to the typical national training syllabus, the best we can hope for is basic control of the machine and rudimentary knowledge of the particular country's "rules of the road". The basic test does not equip new riders with a comprehensive understanding of the hazards they will face and how to address them for their continuous safety.

This is where the role of an Advanced Rider Trainer is fundamental to reducing the number of bikers killed or injured...by more rapidly developing rider skills so they can enjoy a much safer and more rewarding riding experience.

There are many skilled and knowledgeable advanced rider trainers who have chosen to pass on their skills but whose ability to train effectively is diminished for a multitude of reasons. Many know the subject comprehensively, yet somehow fail to communicate it adequately for their students' benefit. This handbook aims to help you avoid the pitfalls so you can interact with your students in a professional, informative and constructive training environment.

As an Advanced Rider Trainer, your involvement must provide a structured programme of rider training to ensure the student is well advised throughout their development and to prepare them for their Advanced Riding Test if that is their goal. You will need to develop the skill to recognise your student's riding ability and any weaknesses they display, if you are to become a highly competent Advanced Rider Trainer. Only then will you be qualified to suggest suitable remedies whilst maintaining their interest and motivation to succeed.

The Advanced Rider Trainer must:
- understand Motorcycle Roadcraft – the Police Rider's Handbook in advanced riding skills and techniques to support their Advanced Rider training programme
- design and deliver a development course, which is structured and sufficiently flexible to meet the needs of the student
- use a variety of training aids to outline the skills required to ride safely, smoothly and under control
- display a high standard of riding skill, willing to demonstrate a skill when required
- identify, prioritise, analyze and rectify riding faults

You are there to help develop the students' skills, impart your knowledge and show how the students' own experience can be used to improve their riding continuously for many years to come.

This Handbook is designed to support you throughout your development on the road to become a knowledgeable and confident Advanced Rider Trainer.

The terminology "Trainer" and "Student" is used throughout this book to distinguish between the role of the person providing the training and the person receiving it. There are other titles or names that are used to make the distinction between these groups of people. It may depend on your personal preference, for example Instructor and Student, or that of your employer or voluntary organisations which may have chosen to define these roles with their own titles. Whatever the choice of terminology you can be assured we are all out to achieve the same thing - impart unrivalled knowledge and expertise to improve rider competence and therefore safety, for themselves and other road users.

We like to recount real life experiences from our own biking careers to re-enforce messages we wish to convey. You are going to find a lot of them throughout this book. We have found that they work really well to get the message across to your students. It also reinforces your ability and willingness to learn from what your senses tell you. If we tell our students what we see, hear, feel and smell it will contribute to everyone's sense of well being when we ride. But if they ever taste the road then they will have fallen off!

We, the authors are UK expatriots who live in Cyprus. We are passionate about motorcycling and "getting it right" otherwise when it goes wrong it will hurt. We are honest and realistic and believe us when we say that we have had our fair share of spills!

Steve Tucker & David Rainford

THIS HANDBOOK

- *Advanced Rider Traininng Organisations*
- *Trainer credibility*
- *Self analysis and Trainer performance*
- *Role of Motorcycle Roadcraft*
- *Introduction to IPSGA*

The contents of this Handbook will provide you with the knowledge and expertise on how to perfect your skills as an Advanced Rider Trainer. It is full of valuable tips and advice to improve your performance as a professional or a skilled volunteer Trainer.

YOUR ROUTE TO BECOMING A SUCCESSFUL TRAINER

To become an Advanced Rider Trainer you should already hold some award or recognition in advanced riding skills which you gained either in the workplace, for example a traffic police officer or with a suitably qualified Trainer at your own expense or with a charitable organisation such as RoSPA (The Royal Society for the Prevention of Accidents) or the IAM (Institute of Advanced Motorists).

The training requires a lot of determination, concentration and commitment, particularly of your time. It is therefore imperative that, to be considered for further training to become an Advanced Rider Trainer, you must continually ride to a high standard in readiness to meet the criteria for acceptance into such a training programme that the different organisations have in place.

Obviously, you must be able to demonstrate advanced riding skills. You will, ideally, also have received comprehensive training and guidance, assessing your suitability, before setting out to become an Advanced Rider Trainer. Hopefully, you will then receive professional training to do so. Your skill and ability must be to the standards of a recognised qualification and the associated test will most likely have contained some theoretical input as well as practice on the road.

It is extremely important to practice your skills. If you do not practice you will lose your edge, not only in how you ride and control your machine but most particularly your own scanning technique. The brain is a muscle that also needs exercise to keep fit. If you have not ridden for some time, you will need to get your brain back up to speed. Do so slowly!

As an Advanced Rider Trainer, you are responsible for providing advice, guidance, mentoring and training of advanced riding techniques to any rider who wishes to be become an advanced rider.

To train someone to ride professionally is a unique and rewarding experience. Advanced Rider training is a skill that has to be learnt, practised and implemented to attain and to perfect your skills to meet the highest professional standards. Thereafter, you must also discipline yourself to regularly review your skills and ability, to increase your knowledge and improve your training abilities.

One of the most important things that you can do as a Trainer is to lead by example, which starts with and continues with, your own development to ensure you become and remain a competent Trainer. The self-development and training you received will help

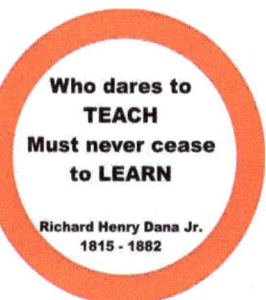

ensure that you acquire the knowledge and practical skills that an Advanced Rider Trainer needs to be successful. In this handbook we focus on developing your communication and training skills to perfect techniques which assist the ease with which your future students can learn from you.

Throughout your development as an advanced rider Trainer, take the opportunities to become a better Trainer by continually reviewing your own performance. At the end of every training session ask yourself:

- What things did I do well?
- What things did I do that could be improved?

How will you empower yourself and improve your own performance? You can do this by making notes of your plan of self-improvement, implement them, bring about change and discuss them with any mentor and your peers.

The UK government has recently recommended those involved with learner rider training to form groups, to share knowledge and techniques, in order to improve the standards of rider training. We would recommend this is also done for those involved with advanced rider training.

First do your homework to find out which is the best course of action for you, whether you wish to do this for a career, in a voluntary capacity or a combination of both. If you proceed, what you are to embark on will be a challenging experience because you will soon realise that you will no longer be riding for yourself alone, but for two (including yourself) or more under your instruction.

The duration and content of any advanced riding course will also vary depending on which organisation you choose to go with.

The one thing that links all UK training organisations together is the fact that they will refer to Motorcycle Roadcraft – The Police Rider's Handbook (ISBN 978978-0-11-708188-8) which is recognised as the definitive book on advanced riding techniques. This is an essential read and must be part of your "toolkit".

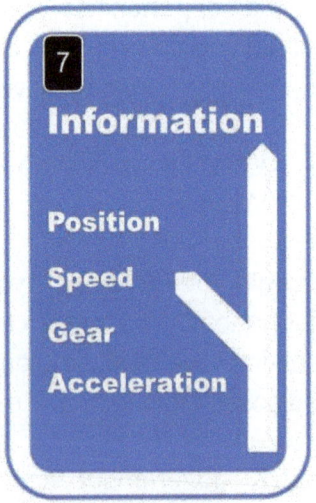

Motorcycle Roadcraft is used by UK police forces to perfect riding skills and standards. The selection process and training of potential motorcyclists, is lengthy and complex. Not everyone who attends one of these courses will pass. There will probably be a dropout rate during the course and failures at test.

Generally, advanced riding courses for the public are not as lengthy, condensed or pressurised as police courses and quite rightly so. But what is expected is that a student can respond, adopt and adapt to the "System of Riding", known as Motorcycle Roadcraft.

In fact you may already possess a copy, as it would have been the point of reference when you trained as an advanced rider.   If you do not, and it is not part of your proposed training package, we recommend that you get a copy.

Without comprehensive knowledge of the contents of Motorcycle Roadcraft, your performance as a Trainer may justifiably be questioned or doubted by your students.   That is not a good position to be in when you wish to portray yourself as a professional Trainer.   You must fully understand the contents of the book and the terminology that is used, for you to confidently explain and display the techniques to your students.

Motorcycle Roadcraft describes the System for riding known by the acronym IPSGA. The five stages for the System of riding are Information, Position, Speed, Gear and Acceleration. However, it does not describe in detail how skills in the use of the System can be acquired or taught to riders. That is the role of the Advanced Rider Trainer and one purpose of this book.

This handbook aims to provide Trainers with guidance in the techniques by which advanced riding skills can be developed in their students. It is up to you to bring Motorcycle Roadcraft to life, much like actors reading a script for a movie, it is up to the director, in this case you, to make your actors performances memorable.

The System is essentially describing how we deal with the road hazards we will encounter. These fall into three categories, namely i) fixed, e.g. traffic signs ii) moving, e.g. other road users and iii) weather. The first stage of riding to the System is Information and there are three phases for this stage, a) Take, e.g. the meaning from your observations, b) Use e.g. changes to your position, speed and gear and c) Give, e.g. signals.

Generally, the contents of Motorcycle Roadcraft are not duplicated in this handbook. Your goal is to perfect your skills as a Trainer. That will come about by using your knowledge and expertise to deliver practical training programmes for riders who are new to advanced riding techniques. However, you will almost certainly need to refer to Motorcycle Roadcraft on occasions, so keep it to hand for briefings before and after a ride.

From the outset, your student should have a good idea of what they wish to achieve with you. They will have made contact directly, responded to an advert or by recommendation, perhaps, by attending a Bike Safe Assessment. Are you offering a one-off experience of several hours or, perhaps, a day of riding or a structured training programme over a period of time? Either way, your time spent with your students must be successful in achieving what he or she wants or expects from you, whether or not they pay for your time.

Our involvement in rider training has confirmed the viewpoint that any advanced rider training is better than no training. But the reality is, a few hours or one day's input of training for a rider wishing to improve their skills, is unlikely to result in them being a proficient advanced rider. That takes time and plenty of practice. A perfected scanning technique, to continually process Information rapidly in a relaxed state of mind, is the key to the rest of the System. It is paramount for rider safety. We are sure you would agree. Realistically, can a rider, new to advanced riding, develop his or her scanning ability to this level of competence in such a short amount of time?

Generally, where time available is limited it is good to introduce scanning and to do your best by giving lots of examples as to how effective it is. Find out from your student what they want to achieve. There may be many aspects of their riding that they wish to improve but, with the time you have allocated to them, you will have to prioritise what can be achieved. It is better to concentrate and perfect one aspect of their ride, than to attempt to correct a multitude of habits that you recognise, but just will not have the time to address. They will appreciate what you have done for them, what their potential is for further development and, who knows, you will probably get repeat business.

A popular way to train in advanced riding skills is to join a credible voluntary charitable organisation, such as the Institute of advanced Motorists (IAM) or The Royal Society for the Prevention of Accidents (RoSPA) with a RoADAR Group. They are spread throughout the UK.

These organisations deliver training by advanced riders, who generally have a lot of advanced motor cycling expertise and a genuine interest in road safety to make riders safer.

For more information on these organisations, contact details can be found on the internet. These voluntary groups generally meet on pre-arranged dates and times to conduct their riding assessments and provide training, which is structured to guide them towards preparing for their advanced riding test.

If this is the environment in which you train, or have a desire to do so, there will probably be a number of training sessions that a member should attend to prepare them for test. This will have been agreed by the Head Office or by a local Committee of the Group.

There are some pre-requisites that the Trainer should establish are in place before riding with a would-be student. This is in addition to having a roadworthy bike, protective helmet and clothing:

- he/she has a full motorcycle driving licence
- he/she has good eyesight
- their level of motorcycle experience on public roads
- they know (UK) road traffic law, road signs, how to make progress and negotiate hazards to the Government test standard
- that they will undergo training/development to fully appreciate the contents of Motorcycle Roadcraft and will be provided with professional feedback on their riding performance

- and most importantly, they have recognised their own need to learn and improve their riding skills

TOOLKIT

Your Trainer's "toolkit" includes more than just a mechanics kit for breakdowns. You should have one, of course, but also a First Aid Kit, maps, Motorcycle Roadcraft, Highway Code, pen and notebook, puncture outfit, radios to communicate with and back-up batteries if necessary,  drinking water, visor cleaner, cable ties, money and phone preferably with a camera facility. Hopefully never needed - an insurance claims form for use in the event of a crash to record details of witnesses, a plan etc.

Our preference is to keep this all in a topbox; our days of riding with a rucksack are long gone.

More and more Trainers are using on board cameras to record the rides of their students. It is also useful to record your own rides for safety purposes, particularly the movement of other road users for evidential purposes if you are ever involved in a crash. *NB: As Advanced Rider Trainers we never use the term "accident" believing there to be no such thing!*

There are plenty of clips on the internet showing how well the cameras can be used to positive effect.

We can vividly remember watching a clip where the student was positioning late on left hand bends and drifting out towards oncoming traffic. Once would have been enough for either of us to have intervened and corrected the riding fault. However, what we witnessed in the video was this behaviour repeated time after time. On one occasion, in our opinion, it was too close for reasonable safety in the presence of an oncoming truck.

There is one overriding factor that a Trainer must consider whenever a camera is used and that is, if a student crashes, you will be first on scene and possess evidence of how it happened. Imagine if the rider in the clip we have just described crashed head on, how would the Trainer have felt, knowing that he or she could have intervened earlier? Then there is, of course, the probability that the video will be viewed by Police who are responsible for recording how the crash happened and apportioning blame.

SPECIAL EMPHASIS - ROUTES AND DIRECTIONS

- *Select routes to meet your training objectives*
- *Learn your routes and the landmarks for direction changes*
- *Practice giving directions without a student – talk out loud to perfect your timing*
- *Practice alternatives in case you are diverted or your student makes a mistake or mishears your instructions*
- *Ride your routes at different times of day to experience different traffic conditions*

We need to emphasise the importance of route planning ahead of any training session so you always provide real time directions on the move. This cannot be stressed highly enough. Training is the reason you are riding with a student. It is NOT navigation.

When training, you do not want to be focused on where you are going. Your attention needs to be directed towards your students. The only way you will achieve this is by making sure that you find and know the routes you will use for training very well.

This means riding them many times at different times of day, whilst observing the typical hazards and practicing giving route instructions in a concise and timely manner.

Ideally, you should have routes that can encompass cities or large towns, villages, single and dual carriageway roads outside of towns where speed limits are higher, uphills, downhills, bends and double apex bends etc. Ultimately, your routes will be governed by what is achievable because of your geographical position, but maximise the potential of your road system to provide your student with as much variation as possible.

Your routes and the hazards along the way should be linked to what the aims and objectives of the assessment or training period are to be. For example, emerging from a minor road to a major road on an incline will need more research to locate than a set of traffic lights.

A good route will develop the student's skills and be very enjoyable at the same time. Also consider riding on different days of the week and times of day to introduce a greater variance in traffic conditions. A circular route is better than the same road to and from where you met your student. You will also have to take into account the distance you will be able to travel within the time allocated to the training session, which should include your recap of any previous session, briefing and de briefing.

You should also try to identify alternate routes which might be needed to deal with obstructions, navigation error on the part of your student or, heaven forbid, incomplete or confusing directions from you as the Trainer! You need to know how to get you and your students back on track and do so without losing their confidence in you.

No training can happen when lost or off route because your attention is elsewhere. Getting back on track becomes the goal which is then a major distraction from all other training activities – observation, feedback, scanning etc will be sacrificed unnecessarily.

You may know your intended route, but can you communicate it with timely directions to a student whilst also observing their performance and maintaining your own safety?

You must know the route and communicate it irrespective of what happens – to you, your student and other road users. Your hazard perception and your communication skills must be excellent to do this consistently. Make it easy on yourself – start by knowing your route and practicing the communication needed to inform your students where you want them to go.

You will not be leading the ride, your student will. He or she will want to know where they are going. The trick with giving directions is to let the person know where you would like them to go in ample time so it does not feel rushed for them and that the direction can be clearly understood and not cause any confusion.

If your command for a change of direction is too early, they will begin to wonder if they have misheard the directions or be distracted trying to look for it and slow down. If your command is too late your student may still want to commit to it. This is a very dangerous situation to be in as your student may well take unnecessary risks to complete the manoeuvre, which could result in loss of control of the bike or a crash. If they do not commit to the command, you will now be off your route and have to re-think your new route, which will distract from your observed ride of the student.

On your routes, look out for landmarks and features at the side of the road to pinpoint where you change direction. This will help greatly with your route planning and communication.

COMMUNICATION ON THE MOVE

- *Radio communication is by far the best*
- *You must allow for slight connection delays before your instructions – use their name*
- *Remember you may be wired to the radio and the bike!*
- *Without radios the training will take longer to complete*

RADIO EQUIPMENT

By far the best way to communicate is with radios. The ideal set up is for the Trainer to be able to transmit and for the student to hear only. There are two reasons for this. Less equipment to buy, install and remove on your student's bikes and two-way conversations are a big distraction to the training you are delivering.

There are many radios on the market to choose from. An important factor in choice is that the equipment has sufficient volume and clarity to be heard above your engine and road noise. Do your own research.

You may wish to have a hard wired system connected to your bike's power source or use rechargeable batteries. This will come down to personal choice and affordability. If you are training paying customers you will be able to offset your purchase costs through future training fees.

For both the Trainer and Student the radio has to be kept in a safe place. Generally, this is in a pocket of a riding jacket. As a Trainer you may wish to have yours fixed to your bike. We prefer the use of a waterproof pouch which is attached to a belt around our waists and is something that can be provided for students to protect your equipment, which is on loan to them.

We have selected Intaride as our preferred provider. (See www.intaride.com)

If you choose a communications system that is wired, you will probably have a push to talk button on your left handlebar. Make sure you can operate it and it does not affect the use of the clutch lever or - BMW riders - your left indicator button. If you have not used this system before be aware that it will take some time to become accustomed to its position and can distract from your view of the road ahead if you look down at it. We mention this fact as every Trainer who has trained with us has always looked down at it in the early stages of use and has had to be advised of their action to prevent it becoming a habit.

It is important to remember that, when the equipment is in use, **you are wired to it**. Never forget to disconnect one or more of your connections before you get off your bike, otherwise you will be in for a surprise.

The only wire coming out of the student's radio will be for the single earpiece. Right or left it makes no difference, the student will have their preference. The earpiece is put into place before the helmet is put on...duh! It will happen and you will laugh about it, as your student looks at you holding their earpiece in their hand.

There are various types of earpieces on the market. They are cheap enough, which is good, as they will not last forever. They can also offer remarkable audio quality if you choose your supplier carefully. The most common types are the ear bud, which sits in the ear. One size does not fit all, so it may be too tight and press on the ear with the helmet on, or too loose and fall out. If it is too loose your ride will be disrupted many times, stopping for the student to put it back in.

Fortunately, there is an easy solution to this problem. Elasticated sports tape has very good adhesive qualities, much better than a plaster. It will not readily separate when placed over the earpiece to hold it in place onto the ear, even under the helmet. The earpiece stays in place, the student hears what you have to say and you can get out of the car park without stopping.

Another common type is the over the ear speaker, which is good for comfort, if an earbud is uncomfortable to use. The best type is a flexible one made of silicone, so it can be stretched over the ear and provides a comfortable fit for most people. Riders come in all sizes and shapes and so do their ears and no matter how much some riders stretch the earpiece, it will not fit and if it did, it would be very constrictive and uncomfortable. By having both sets of earpieces available, you should be able to find the right choice for your students.

In the event that a student has difficulty with either of these earpieces, they can buy a pair of slim fit and cushioned ear pads which will fit in their helmet, either as a permanent fix or secured with Velcro.

Hygiene is very important if the earpieces are rotated among your students. Always remember to clean them after use, before they are re-used. Some students prefer to use their own earpiece(s) which is good if it is compatible with the audio outlet on your radio or they may wish to buy an earpiece from you for personal use.

Voice activated communications that use Bluetooth technology are generally more expensive to buy and equip students with. They also have to be secured to their helmet. If you do choose this type of communication system, you should always start any verbal command with one or two words, before the words you want to be acted upon are spoken. This is because there may be a delay in your transmission as your system activates and the first one or two words will not be received by the student, who may then not act on your instructions. For example, you could say "OK David" and then give your command which should be heard in its entirety.

In the event of communications failure or you do not use a radio communication system, your student will be reliant on receiving visual information from you. The plus side to this style of training is that your students will be extremely competent in using their mirrors from an early stage and throughout their development with you.

Before setting off you must give a briefing and tell the student that you will ride behind them to the offside so that they will see your indicators in their offside mirror. Then say:

> "When I indicate right, take the next road on the right".
> "When I indicate left, take the next road on the left".
> "At crossroads or roundabouts, if I do not signal, go straight ahead at the junction".
> "At the end of the assessment or if I need you to stop before then, I will overtake you and indicate left for us to pull up in a safe and convenient place".
> "If we get separated, stop and wait for me at the side of the road. If I cannot locate you, I will return to the last place you saw me and meet you there".

This technique of giving directions will dramatically reduce your choice of route as there cannot be any confusion as to the direction you wish your student to take. Imagine approaching a roundabout which has five exits, three of which are off to the right and you want your student to take the fourth exit. It isn't going to happen.

We stress again - "PLAN YOUR ROUTES VERY CAREFULLY".

There is also another aspect of training that you should consider if you do not use radios. The training of your students will take longer to complete for reasons which will become evident as you read more of this book.

GIVING DIRECTIONS

- *Always use the student's name before every instruction – grabs their attention*
- *Keep instruction "short and sweet"*
- *Use the clock face directions at roundabouts*
- *Practice all instructions and directions aloud to yourself before using on a student*

When you are ready to ride, a good way of attracting the attention of your student over the radio is to use their first name before any command. It works exceptionally well and alerts them to your next command. Speak clearly and a little slower than you would if you were in a conversation. For example, when you are both ready to ride you could say, "David, ride on when you're ready please" or "David, when leaving the car park I'd like you to turn left please".

Whilst riding at any speed and giving directions over a two way radio, remember that the more you say, the more time you will need to say what is needed. This will impact on the amount of distance you have to get your command across. You must ensure that there is always enough distance between you and the point when you want your student to change direction.

KEEP IT SIMPLE, LESS SAID = BETTER.
YOU WILL HAVE MORE TIME AND DISTANCE TO WORK WITH.

Let's consider the following examples of how time, speed and distance will impact on your verbal commands.

You say, "David, at the end of the road, turn right" – the command takes 3 seconds.

If you say, "David, when you get to the end of the road, I would like you to turn right please" the command takes 5. 5 seconds.

The difference is 2. 5 seconds, which at 30mph means you need an extra 33 metres of road distance to communicate your command.   That's the length of 3 Double Decker Buses!

Remember to use the student's name before the command is given to guarantee that a) you have attracted their attention and b) any glitches in sound transmission do not overlap with your commands.

Here are some more examples of simple commands you might like to get into the habit of using.

"David, follow the road ahead" – 2. 2 seconds
"David, at the traffic lights, follow the road ahead / turn right / left" – 3. 3 seconds
"David, take the next road on the right / left" – 3 seconds
"David, at the end of the road turn right / left" – 3 seconds
"David, take the second road on the right / left, this is the first (as you approach it) – 4. 4 seconds

"David, pull up on the left in a safe and convenient place" – 3. 6 seconds

"David, move to the right / left hand lane" – 2. 4 seconds

"David, at the roundabout turn right, the third exit" – 4 sec

In the next chapter, we provide a time, speed and distance table which shows how these simple instructions take a varying distance on the road, depending on you and your student's speed. 3 seconds being approximately 42 metres at 50kph (30mph) and 83 metres at 100kph (62mph). The maximum length of an articulated truck and trailer on UK roads is 16. 5 metres so that is 2 ½ truck lengths at town speeds and 5 on the open road!

DIRECTIONS FOR NEGOTIATING A ROUNDABOUT

Imagine the roundabout as a clock face. You always approach a roundabout at 6 o'clock. Any exit after 12 o'clock is a right turn.

So, by knowing the layout of roundabouts with any number of exits and using this technique you can see them as they would appear on a clock face and you can confidently identify the exit you want the student to leave by and whether the command is to go left, straight ahead or right. This technique removes all confusion for your students.

So at any roundabout, directions might be:

"David, at the roundabout turn left, the first exit" or

"David, at the roundabout follow the road straight ahead, the first/second/third exit" etc or

"David, at the roundabout turn right, the first/second/third exit etc".

Now you have the basics for giving instructions on the move commit them to memory. It is so much easier for a Trainer to have a routine rather than trying to think what you want to say on the move. You may know where you are going but your thought processes will be working hard to put into words what needs to be said and those precious seconds lost could delay the timing of your directions, making them feel rushed for your student.

By now, we hope you will have realised that your communications skills must be perfected before you go near a real student! Lack of clarity, precision, hesitancy or bad timing will require greater mental attention and cost you time and distance. This is a distraction for you and a lack of your attention to your student's performance. If you recognise that your own performance is lacking, chances are so will your student!

TIME SPEED AND DISTANCE

- *Developing hazard perception*
- *Changing awareness into anticipation*
- *Using anticipation for preparation and proactive riding*
- *Reinforce IPSGA*

The skill in training a rider to an advanced level is for you to be the master of time, speed and distance and for your student to mirror this skill. Each parameter is related to the other two.

Time Speed Distance Chart									
	Distance Travelled in...								
Speed	1 sec	2 sec	3 sec	4 sec	5 sec	10 sec		...to Stop	
kph			Metres				Think	Brake	Total
30	8	17	25	33	42	83	6	6	12
50	14	28	42	56	69	139	9	14	23
65	18	36	54	72	90	181	12	24	36
80	22	44	67	89	111	222	15	38	53
100	28	56	83	111	139	278	18	55	73
110	31	61	92	122	153	306	21	75	96
mph			Feet					...to Stop	
20	29	59	88	117	100	293	20	20	40
30	44	88	132	176	150	440	30	46	76
40	59	117	176	235	200	587	39	79	118
50	73	147	220	293	250	733	49	125	174
60	88	176	264	352	300	880	59	180	240
70	103	205	308	411	350	1027	69	246	315
kph to m	0.27778								
mph to ft	1.46667								

You and your student are always travelling in the present time with the future in front of you and the past behind you.

Relying on instinct and reaction time is not good enough to keep safe all of the time on the road. You both need to be proactive to remain safe in all circumstances and able to ride at speeds appropriate for the circumstances. It is better to anticipate hazards rather than react to them, which may be too late. You both need to see into the future and not react when you get there. Anticipation allows both of you to respond and be ready for hazards and developing situations so that you arrive at what is ahead of you, the future, in the right position, at the right speed and in the right gear, ready for the next set of future hazards. If neither you nor your student has implemented the System by the time you arrive at the hazard, then your efforts are too late! The hazard is now in the past.

The geometry, surface conditions, lighting, weather, vegetation and street furniture present illusions and distortions for the riders senses. Now add other road users and you have a range of hazards to be addressed, no matter what your speed. Your role as Trainer is to help the student develop a reliable sense of hazard assessment to be able to ride at an appropriate speed with confidence.

As a Trainer, your view of the future has to allow for the time your student needs to prepare themselves in sufficient time and distance before arriving at the hazard. You must equip your student to be able to do all his or her braking, gear changes and position adjustments before arriving at the hazard. If the work is not done by the time of reaching the hazard there is potential for serious error or a crash.

Observations and scanning technique are skills which really let a biker "read" the road to set their machine up correctly. Luck is not a skill, you are just postponing the day of reckoning if you rely on it.

SCANNING

- *Physiology – vision drops*
- *"Eyes Up" – the constant challenge*
- *Head and eye movement*

Our vision naturally drops as we look ahead.   We humans, which includes bikers, are biologically programmed to process images at walking speed or at our maximum running speed. This is part of the flight or fight reflex. We also tend to focus on specific elements of the image we see. Is there a threat? This processing takes time, so we are inclined to stare at them. This behaviour works well when we walk and run but when we ride at speeds greater than the human brain and mind is designed for, we must be much better with our observation techniques.

Staring is extremely dangerous for any rider because our hands naturally respond to where our eyes are looking! That is how we can catch a ball or swing a tennis racket. Look where you want to go! If we concentrate on what we want to avoid *we will hit it*!

When riding, not only must we look further ahead than is natural, we must also turn our heads to look left and right for the hazards that may not yet be in our peripheral vision. Human peripheral vision is more sensitive to motion than our straight ahead vision. Therefore, by moving the eyes and the head, we also make ourselves more sensitive to things that are in front of us. Advanced riding requires us to train our eyes and our heads to move more than is natural so that our brains are better able to recognise, in less time, what our eyes see.

This technique is called scanning.

By looking as far ahead as possible to assess the far, middle and near distance, we will better recognise the hazards in order to prioritise them and use IPSGA to make sure we have a safe, smooth and controlled ride. The student is fully prepared and has increased time to process the information and act accordingly. Riding then becomes more relaxed, comfortable and pleasurable because the student will find there are few, if any, surprises.

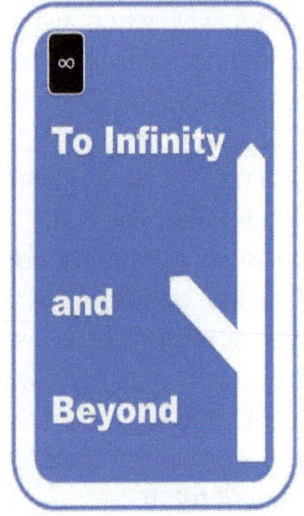

Without training it is extremely difficult to scan effectively. A rider has to experience numerous situations and receive feedback from a professional Trainer to become proficient in scanning and to keep their vision raised consistently.

As a Trainer, you will have to continually encourage your students to scan effectively. In the early stages of development their vision will continually drop and they will miss hazards, go off line in bends and generally ride slower than is necessary for safety. Unless you, as their Trainer, pick up on the clues which tell you their vision has dropped, you will not be able to help develop your students' scanning ability. This skill will ensure they can become a proactive rider, rather than reacting to hazards immediately in front of them, for which they will have very little time.

You can develop your students scanning ability by using the following training techniques which have been proven to be effective in achieving efficient observation skills.

i) Every time you both enter a new road or exit a bend, scan ahead as far as is possible – "to infinity and beyond" (courtesy of Buzz Lightyear). Identify a feature that is at the limit of your vision and tell your student over the radio. Your students will then try to identify it and you will have provided a point of comparison with how far they are looking compared to you. This will force them to start to look further ahead if they were not already doing so. You can be certain that they will not miss the near or middle distance hazards but you will also observe that your student slows down until they become comfortable with the new technique they are trying to master.

ii) Use the word "scan" frequently and whenever you get your student to look ahead, to the left, right, over, under and through any objects – vehicles, trees etc.

iii) It is very common for vision to drop in a bend. Use the words "eyes up" over and over again as they ride the bend to assess the limit and exit points.   Watch how they start to improve their position in the bend and their acceleration sense, both on approach and as they recognise the movement of the limit point and the exit. Remember, you may have to say this for many bends until you are satisfied the students vision remains raised to correctly assess the limit and exit point in bends.

iv) Keep the students' eyes up, scanning continuously, by referring to what you, the Trainer, can see at the extremities of your vision. This feedback will identify to the students how well they are scanning in comparison to you. Always be alert to symptoms that your student's vision has dropped, for example incorrect road position and poor acceleration sense, in order to correct their scanning technique.

HOW TO ENGAGE WITH YOUR STUDENTS

- *The Learning Journey*
- *Grabbing your student's attention*
- *Your focus on the student*
- *Helping students retain information to learn*
- *Emotions*
- *Calmness & self-control*
- *Being reliable*
- *Patience and understanding*

FROM INCOMPETENCE TO MASTERY

All of us are different in how we acquire information and knowledge. If everyone learned the same way, we could just give everyone a copy of Motorcycle Roadcraft and tell them to get on with it.

Why have your students come to you for training?

Most likely it started with an "Aha" moment and a growing **awareness** - possibility of knowledge and improvement – that some patterns/problems in their riding could be life threatening and need to be fixed. To this add **motivation** – a near death experience, wife or girlfriend, insurance, spare time etc. and **interest** - desire to know more (about advanced rider skills), if not yet to do it. Then finally you get a new student when he or she decides to do an **exploration**

– and wants to find out how to go about improving his or her knowledge and skills.

Generally your students will be on step No. 2 – they are aware of their own shortcomings on a motorcycle and want to improve.

Advanced rider training is not just about providing knowledge. Advanced Rider Training places a huge learning staircase in front of your students. They must adjust to the use of speed and think through their actions to co-ordinate the use of their eyes, hands and feet to ride a bike safely on the road.

Your job as Trainer is to make their experience as easy, enjoyable and especially painless as possible.

How?

GRAB THEIR ATTENTION

Your students will vary in their riding abilities. You will certainly discover that, at times, your students will not know anything at all about a particular topic, so it will have to be taught from the beginning.

The first thing a Trainer must do for every training session is to get and keep, the attention of the students. Get them involved from the outset of every ride you do with them. Find out what motivates and inspires them so they understand why the training you provide is important to them. When you get this right, you will have keen and enthusiastic students.

BE FOCUSED ON YOUR STUDENTS

When you are giving training, your focus needs to be 100% on your students and their training requirements. Ensure that you are putting all of the attention on your students. It is not about you, it is about your student's performances.

RETAINING INFORMATION

To be an effective Trainer, your own training information needs to be presented in a variety of ways because it helps the student to maintain a keen interest for the topic being discussed. Briefings can include written words, diagrams, examples of real life situations and a demonstration of an exercise in readiness for the practical riding challenges for your students. Try to obtain examples from your students which will be personal and pertinent to assist retention of what they learn. Examples can be taken from their ride to meet you that day or an occasion since you last met. These might include times they anticipated a situation appropriately or another road user did something potentially dangerous but for which they were prepared. It could be as simple as an oncoming vehicle glimpsed through the trees before arriving at a bend enabling the student to adjust position appropriately.

Without a mixture of techniques for every session it can become boring and any topic then has the potential not to be fully understood.

With all the information you are giving students, you must provide time to look back on their achievements and allow them to ask questions. You will also need to ask students questions to confirm their understanding of the subject being discussed and be open and supportive if you need to prompt them in their answer.

Something that is brought home to us time after time from the people we have ridden with is that they hear one of our voices in their heads, encouraging and supporting them when riding alone or out in front with no radio communication from us to guide them. Our students find this very reassuring, are able to correct themselves in the knowledge that the techniques have been assimilated and the self correction is now part of their psyche. The retention of training information, techniques and skills has been a phenomenal success.

EMOTIONS

> ## "People may forget what you said but they will never forget how you made them feel."
> *Maya Angelou 1928 - 2014*

People have feelings and emotions when learning something new. Anything negative will have a dramatic effect on their performance. Encouragement will help them work harder to get it right and give them a feel good effect. It is therefore important to recognise and understand the body language of your students. This provides you with visual clues as to how you are communicating with your student, how they feel about it and how you can respond.

A lot of your students will, ordinarily, be extremely confident. They may have a wealth of lifetime experiences from their workplace and private lives, in what they have done and how they socialise, which make them the confident person you see before you.

However, during training they may be out of their comfort zone and whilst they will try to be calm and rational, it is quite possible there will be moments when they will be nervous, anxious and lacking in confidence. As a Trainer you should be prepared to plan for the emotions that accompany learning. To be an effective Trainer you cannot remain quiet and unsupportive. You must deal with any concerns to dispel any doubts and to promote increased confidence in your students and belief in you.

CALMNESS AND SELF-CONTROL

The common factor with all your students is that they want to learn how to be advanced riders. After that, there is no similarity between their characters and how they will behave or react to your training.

For a variety of reasons, some people will be a major challenge to your patience. Ask any Advanced Rider Trainer about their experiences and they will recount some humorous stories but they also have some horrendous ones too. You must always act professionally. You must not get stressed, lose your temper or raise your voice with a student. Do not jeopardise your credibility, wait until you have an appropriate moment to yourself and then let it all out.

RELIABILITY

I hate being late but I am so good at it

You must ensure that you are always fully prepared and ready to train at all times. Punctuality is fundamental to ensuring you are not under stress or forgetting what needs to be done. For example, if you forget your sunglasses you will spend the rest of the day struggling with the bright sunlight. It is that much harder to see and so reduces your speed unnecessarily. You may therefore also be holding your student back. How can you then undertake a training session on overtaking safely?

PATIENCE AND UNDERSTANDING

Not everyone is going to get it right first time or even the second or third time.

You must be able to ask yourself "Is there a better way for me to make myself understood to help the student complete the task asked of them"? We call it the "adapt or die" technique. It can happen to you at any moment, even on the move.

For whatever reason, the student apparently cannot, or will not, respond to you. You must have the ability to recover immediately and not lose the moment.

Change your approach... *adapt* or the opportunity to recover is lost... *or die.*

Let us see how this works. One recollection is riding with a student who had been briefed on the use of gears to better control speed on descents and bends. We left a mountain village and our route down the mountain was intended to put it all into perspective. The ride started off well but as the descent became steeper and the bends tighter, the student's speed lessened and he was more upright. He was also braking on entering bends. The initial assessment was that he was riding in too high a gear.

The Trainer radioed to him, "Select third gear". The next bend was ridden in the same style as described above. The Trainer then said, "Nod your head if you are in third gear". The student shrugged his shoulders; clearly he did not know what gear he was in.

If he continued to ride down the mountain in this fashion nothing would have been achieved by the training session. Alternatively the Trainer could have stopped the ride and had a question and answer session followed by a revised briefing. Better still the Trainer could have recovered on the move. So *adapt,* save the training session or lose or interrupt it, which is to *die.*

On a long straight, during the ride above, the Trainer said "Go up through your gears until you stop, nod your head when you have done this". A couple of seconds later he nodded his head. The Trainer said "You are in gear six". Another good trait for an Advanced Rider Trainer is to know when to state the obvious. The Trainer said, "Go down one gear – five, go down one gear – four, go down one gear – three". Now the student knew what gear he was in so the training would then be effective. It was also easier to go into second gear and back into third and know which gear he was in.

At the next stop the student was thoroughly pleased with his riding experience and smiling from ear to ear and said he "didn't know that biking could be so much fun". His bike did not have a gear indicator, so he did not know what gear he was riding in when he was first radioed and did not know whether to go up or down the gears. The student reported that he had been in fifth gear, as it only took one gear change to go no further. The Trainer's assessment had been correct.

Remember, if you do not adjust to your students' needs they will be slow to progress, they will lack confidence and it may make them doubt your ability to train them how to ride to an advanced standard.

- *Diplomacy and sense of humour*
- *Keeping an open mind*
- *Honesty*
- *Self study*
- *Listening*
- *Questioning*
- *Encouragement & support*
- *Tips to monitor and support progress*

DIPLOMACY AND SENSE OF HUMOUR

Tact and diplomacy will keep your students happy.

Imagine what your students would think of you if you say things like "That overtake was absolute rubbish, get it right next time" or "How many times do I have to tell you how to do it properly"? It is far better to think before you speak.

Humour is good to calm people down and will reduce stress for your student and you. If there is an opportunity to make a Student laugh take advantage of it. Training that is fun and enjoyable is more effective and memorable too.

AN OPEN MIND

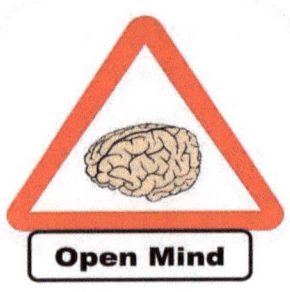

As an Advanced Rider Trainer you may know very little about any of your students before you meet them for the first time. You cannot afford to hold any prejudices or be discriminatory in any way. Treat everyone the way you would wish to be treated yourself and you will both enjoy the training experience.

HONESTY

First be honest with yourself about your own ability as a rider. It takes only one misrepresentation of the truth to jeopardise your reputation and integrity. Remember your students will already have riding experience and possibly strong opinions on how a bike should be ridden. You may even be criticised or at least challenged, on some aspect of training, which you will then need to clarify without confusing your students.

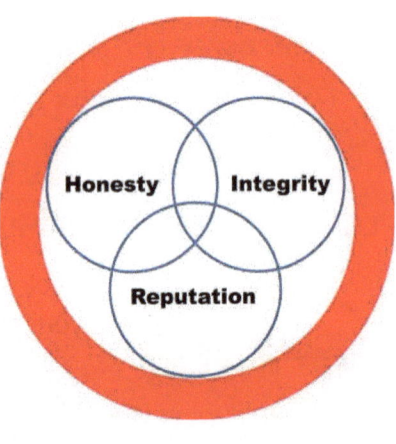

You will ride with some who think they are capable of riding much faster than you. You may find this a challenge as, although they might have the practical machine control and bravery to ride too quickly, they may not have the techniques perfected to do so safely. You will need to modify their behaviour by demonstrating that they are not making proper allowance for other factors, such as road conditions and stopping within the distance they can see to be clear.

They may be cutting the bend rather than maintaining an outside line when it would be more appropriate for the bend in question.

Your students will be expecting the very best in terms of training and feedback. Be accurate with your comments, actions and instructions. There may necessarily be an element of confrontation. You will need to demonstrate that you are giving sound, reasoned and evidence based guidance and you are not simply expressing a personal opinion. For example, you may need to accept that the racing line would be quicker but it would not be as safe. You must robustly question whether the rider is recognising the risks he is taking by not identifying all the hazards he is exposing himself to.

BE PREPARED TO STUDY A LOT AND BE SELF-MOTIVATED

Before, during and after you qualify as an Advanced Rider Trainer keep up to date with training development and training methods, legislation and perhaps seek to obtain additional qualifications. Your training skills need to keep pace with technology such as ABS, linked brakes and traction control. What effect will electric motorcycles have on the way you train?

Until the age four or five we learned by listening and observing the world around us. At school we received our formal education and the teachers often told us to "sit down and be quiet." We were then expected to learn through reading and writing. We had no further training in the art and two-way process of listening, unless we were very lucky.

When you are the Trainer dealing with adults, **listening to them,** before offering help to solve problems, is probably one of the most important skills you will need.

As you train them, you need to learn to listen with real focus and re-think any predisposition you may have for instant judgements and immediate opinions. You also need to be listening with your eyes, not just hearing the words but truly understanding the communication of their body language. As an Advanced Rider you know how to interpret vehicle "body language", a similar skill is required of you with your students.

QUESTIONING

Anyone can ask questions. When you are a Trainer you need to use powerful and short questions to test the knowledge and ability of your student. The questions must be:

- Understood by the student to give an answer based on their knowledge
- Able to improve the learning of the student being trained
- Able to move the student forward towards an achievement for the lesson ahead
- Open rather than closed. Closed questions are those, which can be answered by a simple Yes or No. Open questions are those which require more thought and more than a simple one word answer and will test the knowledge of your students more effectively.

Typically these questions begin with what, why, when, how, where or who, as in Rudyard Kipling's "The Elephant's Child"

I keep six honest serving-men
They taught me all I knew
Their names are What and Why and When
And How and Where and Who

Examples of closed questions:

- "Did you check your mirror?" - Yes or No, end of story
- "Did you see the new speed limit sign?" - Yes or No, again end of story

Examples of an open - ended question:

- "**What** did you observe in your mirrors?"
- "**Why** did you indicate at the last junction?"
- "**When** would you use your horn?"
- "**How** do you check the oil level on your bike?"
- "**Where** did the speed limit change?
- "**Who** services your brakes?

ENCOURAGE AND SUPPORT YOUR STUDENTS

Be positive with your students. A good way to deal with a problem that is causing someone difficulty is to start with a positive remark. Once you have their interest, you can then advise them how to make it better. Conclude your feedback with another positive remark.

The table highlights some of the enablers and blockers so that you will know what to do more of and what to avoid, particularly the post-ride feedback and reviews.

For example:

"Your riding has been good today; you've been positioning yourself very well. I know that there is a lot going on when you're riding, but you must remember to keep checking your mirrors. I know you understand why and when you should check them, but you will have to work a bit harder to remember to do them. Get that right and you will continue to improve your riding".

Enablers of Learning	Blockers of Learning
they can recognise their own progress - new/improved knowledge and/or skills	the enablers in the left column are missing or too weak
they are provided with frequent recaps and feedback (essential)	incompatibility with their Trainer
they are given a proper briefing at the start and a thorough debriefing at the end of each session	they are on the wrong machine (type, capacity, size or weight)
they are having a fun and enjoyable experience	they have too low a base competence/insecurity
which is also an engaging experience	they do not fit in with the group - incompatibility/mismatch
	they do not get special attention when they need it

You can also help them to make changes by being firm and assertive to correct faults that keep being repeated. If you do not mention their faults, your students will either not recognise them or think they do not matter sufficiently for you to mention them and these traits will become habits which will be much harder to rectify.

Usually, any student can be bought back to reality by asking the question "If you do that on your test, what will the Examiner do?" So to summarise, as a Trainer you need:

- an excellent understanding of your subject
- the ability to speak clearly, be understood and to listen to others
- the ability to offer students opportunities to learn through participation and action
- flexibility and an ability to easily adapt to the needs of your students
- a willingness to experiment with new ideas
- the ability to learn fast and to learn from your own mistakes
- the desire to help others to learn
- the ability to create an atmosphere of openness and trust with your students
- the ability to plan and implement their training needs
- regular evaluation of your work and success
- an ability to cope and learn when things do not go according to plan
- to be organised in all aspects of training and precise in fulfilling your tasks

TIPS TO MONITOR AND SUPPORT PROGRESS

Every training session must:

- start with a review of the previous training session, if relevant
- include a briefing for the current session
- provide feedback during the session
- provide a de-brief at the conclusion of the session
- result in a verbal agreement from the student that they will practice the riding skills necessary to move on in readiness for their next training session

BRIEFINGS

- *How adults learn – both tutor and student*
- *The Kolb Learning Circle model*
- *Preparing a brief and de-brief – keeping them short*
- *Riding behind a student*

LEARNING/TRAINING CIRCLE

You will be taking your students on many physical journeys. However, there is also the metaphysical journey of learning…you must train them through their discouragement, out of bad habits and into new forms of behaviour and the associated new mind set.

The route map for this journey is illustrated in the diagram overleaf; it is an alternative representation of the staircase shown earlier.

Everyone is different. Some understand, and then do: others do to enable themselves to understand.

Motorcycling is a practical skill and each ride can be a unique learning and development opportunity.

The Kolb Learning Cycle describes this. It provides the context for you to effectively apply the tools in your Trainer's toolkit to help you to understand what is happening for your students. David Kolb (1984) provided one of the most useful descriptive models to explain the adult learning process. Somewhat earlier "Involve me and I will understand" was attributed to Confucius in 450BC!

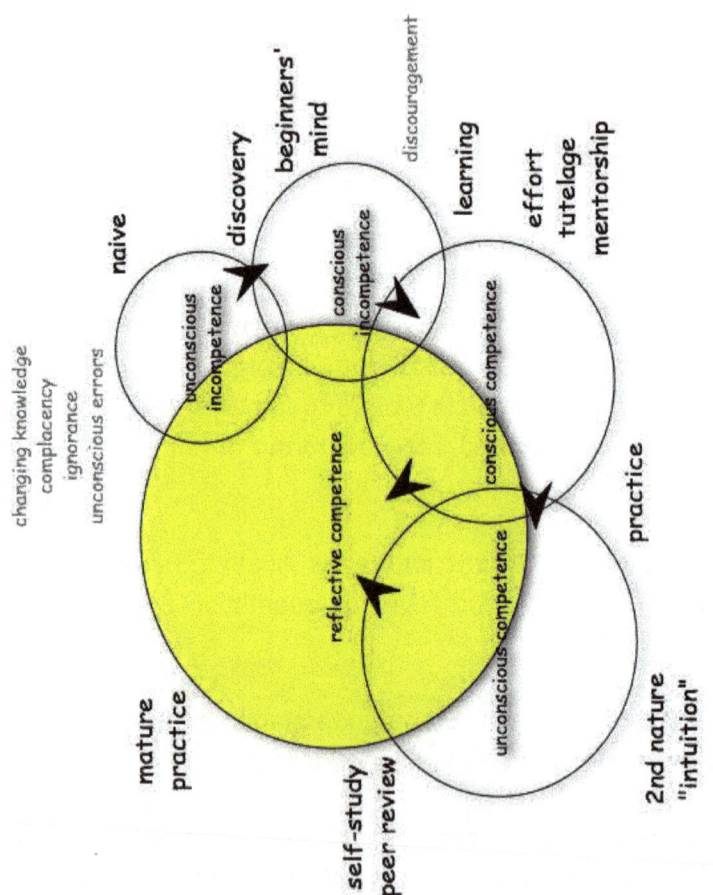

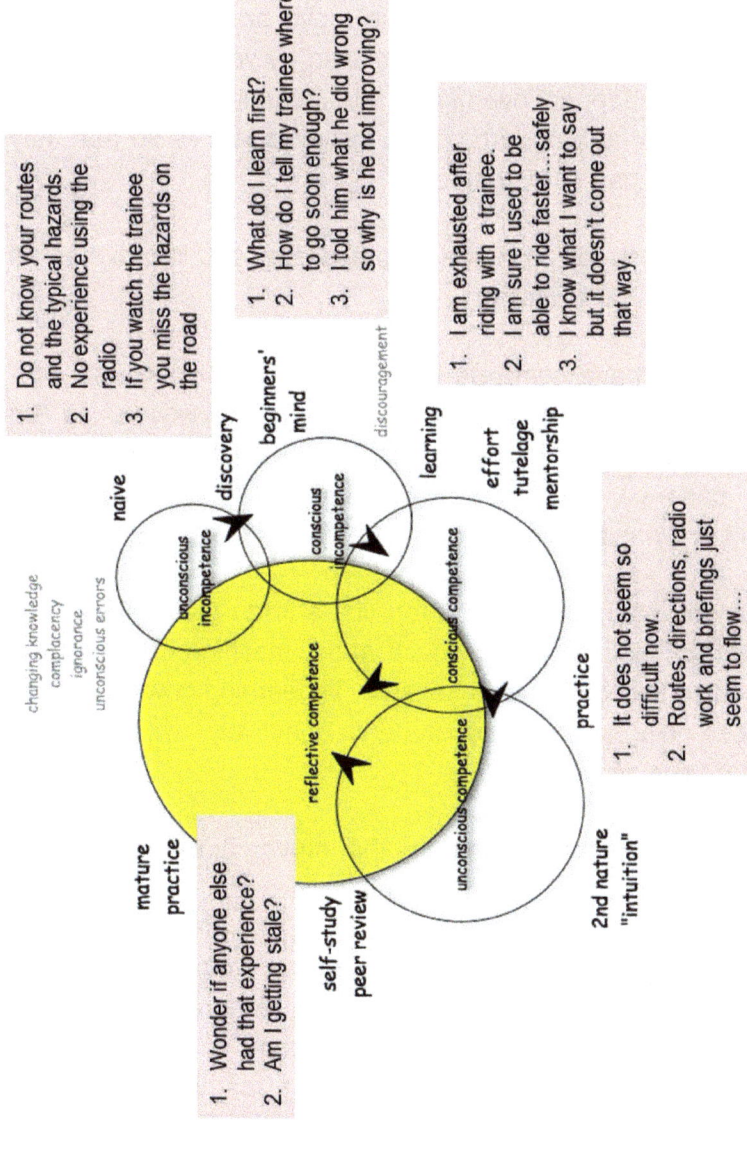

1. Do not know your routes and the typical hazards.
2. No experience using the radio
3. If you watch the trainee you miss the hazards on the road

1. What do I learn first?
2. How do I tell my trainee where to go soon enough?
3. I told him what he did wrong so why is he not improving?

1. I am exhausted after riding with a trainee.
2. I am sure I used to be able to ride faster...safely
3. I know what I want to say but it doesn't come out that way.

1. It does not seem so difficult now.
2. Routes, directions, radio work and briefings just seem to flow...

1. Wonder if anyone else had that experience?
2. Am I getting stale?

changing knowledge
complacency
ignorance
unconscious errors

naive

discovery

beginners' mind

discouragement

learning

effort
tutelage
mentorship

unconscious incompetence

conscious incompetence

conscious competence

reflective competence

conscious competence

unconscious competence

practice

2nd nature "intuition"

mature practice

self-study
peer review

The outer circles represent what is happening out on the road (experience) and with you the Trainer as you give briefings, then feedback on the move and at post ride de-briefings. This has to be assimilated by your students and it does not happen overnight...well actually it does, as the subconscious brain processes the experiences so that they become a part of the person.

You will also follow the same process as you improve as an Advanced Rider Trainer!

You may have complete mastery and be at one with your machine "**as an advanced rider**". However, as an "Advanced Rider Trainer" you start as a novice, learning how to pass on your "Zen Master" skills as effectively and efficiently as possible.

For you as Trainer, when you first start to give training, the outer circles are not so much about machine handling and reading the road and its hazards, as learning how to transfer those riding skills to your students effectively, which requires new skills on your part.

Routes, communications on the move, briefings and de-briefings all need to be mastered.

A very simple four step diagram of the process is overleaf. You do something, reflect on the experience, draw a conclusion and learn something from it, then plan or experiment a little before applying the learning to create a new but better experience.

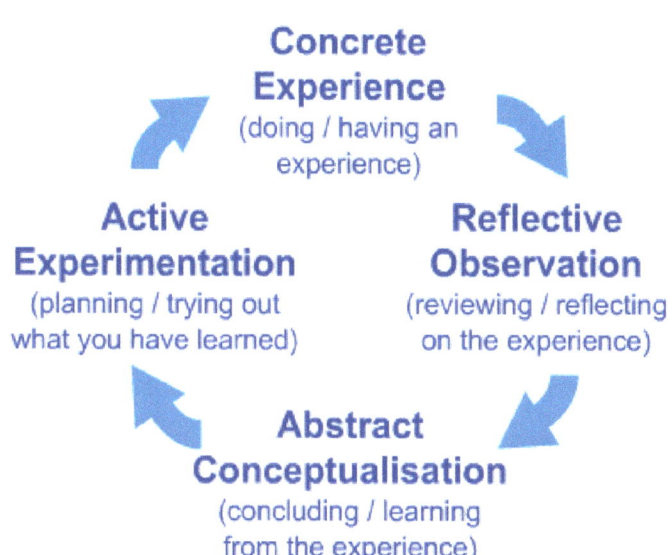

Concrete Experience
(doing / having an experience)

Reflective Observation
(reviewing / reflecting on the experience)

Abstract Conceptualisation
(concluding / learning from the experience)

Active Experimentation
(planning / trying out what you have learned)

An example might be your student entering a right hand bend on the crown of the road and seeing an oncoming vehicle rather late, forcing the student to adjust position and/or brake, thus having an uncomfortable experience. Reflecting on what happened, assisted by your feedback, will lead your student to recognise he should be further over to the left to improve his view. He would then be encouraged to try this and discover a much better riding experience in right hand bends in future. In detail, the reflection might have included aspects of his vision, reading of the road or even use of the rear brake in circumstance where speed must be lost but stability is essential.

THE IMPORTANCE OF BRIEFINGS AND DE-BRIEFINGS

Although briefing is a part of communication, there is a formality about doing so in a training context which can greatly assist the learning process.

Introduction of any training topic is best dealt with by a briefing, which should be accurate and, emphasis on the "brief", not too long.   Once your briefing is complete, it is good to ask questions to ensure your student has understood what has been said and what the student will be doing.   If any detail needs to be repeated or explained differently, you now have the opportunity to do so.   End the briefing with a recap of the topic.

As a Trainer you should find the next section helps you to better appreciate how we all learn differently and what you need to do as Trainer to make the learning effective for all your students.

HOW TO PREPARE A BRIEFING - THE GOLDEN RULES

- As Trainer you must have a complete understanding, knowledge and experience of dealing with the topic you have chosen.
- Keep it short in content; you can always add extra input during the training sessions.
- Know what the aims and objectives are for the training session.
- Remember, do not set training objectives too high, or to be unachievable, in the time you have allocated to the session.
- Compare the skill level required to pass a driving test for the topic you are training and then consider the

additional skills an advanced rider should possess for the topic. Knowing the differences, write down your ideas - you will be better placed to explain what the differences are - why do you do it differently - what are the pros and cons - put them a logical briefing order to be easily understood.

- What are the important factors that must be covered before you ride?
- Do you need visual aids? Always have a notepad and pen to hand in briefings.
- Make sure it is a question and answer session – keep your student involved – they do have experience and a viewpoint.
- Get your student to feedback to you to confirm that they fully understand what they will be doing.
- Be prepared to change your planned training session in the light of experiences which your students might bring to you since your last ride together. You want to build on their receptive frame of mind. (Adapt or die!)
- Finally, keep it simple!

> **"To fail to prepare is to prepare to fail!"**
> (Benjamin Franklin)

GIVING A DE-BRIEF

This is an art and it is well worth taking time to perfect what you want to say at the end of the ride. We have witnessed many Trainers who just cannot get this right; struggling to find the right approach or the right choice of words to use. They get lulled or distracted into talking about matters which aren't really beneficial for a de-brief. You will know if this happens to you because your student will be direct and ask you to tell them how you think they did. If this happens to you re-think your de-brief style to get back on track with what needs to be said.

The importance of offering words of praise for the good parts of the ride cannot be emphasised enough. So many Trainers do not do this and their demeanour comes across as uncaring or disinterested. That is not a good way to part company until the next time you meet. Make sure your student leaves on a high by complimenting them on their efforts.

At the end of the ride it is very important that you let your students know how they have performed. We like to open up a conversation with something like, "Well done, you did well. I enjoyed the ride, did you?" Listen carefully to what is said to you. Tell them what you saw. Give examples or use your pad and pen to help you describe better what you wish to say. Tell the student what was good about the ride, what needs improvement and how they can practice at it until you next meet with them.

Finish by letting them know what they will be doing next time you meet.

TIME TO RIDE

Riding a motorcycle is a very complex procedure in which to become skilled. Think about it, like a musician, riders have to use their eyes, hands and feet, very often at the same time. The brain simultaneously has to process everything the eyes see. Put into perspective, how many other human activities can you think of where this happens…all at speed! Even the fastest musicians remain more or less in one place.

Having a bike licence does not mean someone is a good rider. The Certificate of Basic Training (CBT) in the UK provides a good kick start, but after that further professional training is not a requirement in readiness for a test. Many riders teach themselves how to ride. If they are fortunate, they will pass their test. Dependant on age, other riders will undertake a direct access course and in all probability, opt for some professional training.

But even this is insufficient to adequately equip riders with the skill and expertise to handle a motor bike safely. It does not necessarily need to be high powered either for the rider to be killed, or severely injured, in a crash. Unfortunately, the very high death rate of riders and the main reasons for their crashes is rider error. **Generally, bikers in the UK have a higher mortality rate than active servicemen in war zones**.

Advanced rider training is not difficult to do. Let's keep it very simple. As an Advanced Rider Trainer, you will have acquired an immense amount of knowledge and displayed your skills leading up to and during, your advanced test. When you become a Trainer, you move from being in front of a Trainer to following behind a Student, which is a totally different experience.

A student must hold a full driving licence for the type of motorcycle they use.

The motorcycle must be roadworthy, insured, taxed and have a test certificate if needed. Students must wear a protective crash helmet. Generally, that is the only item of protection equipment that legislation compels. It is up to you and your professionalism, to advise riders on what other protective and weatherproof equipment is required and acceptable to you prior to any on road training being given. You will probably have strong views on what you wear and what your expectations are from others. What are the minimum standards of motorcycle attire that you will accept from those you are about to train? Will a lack of wet weather gear, for example, cause the early termination of, what could otherwise have been, valuable inclement weather training?

You are now the one observing, not the one being observed. And that is a skill you have to perfect for your own safety. Always do your own ride. The student should be in your field of vision but, if you focus too long and stare at the student, you will sacrifice your own scanning technique.

Think about your following distance and position because, if you do not, your view of the road ahead will be obstructed by your student. Worse still is that you may be caught out unawares when a student brakes or backs off the gas and you find yourself having to take avoiding action or swerve around them and pass them, to avoid running into them. What impression does that leave on a student?

COMPETENCE FINGERPRINT

- *A shorthand means to review your students*
- *Attitude first*
- *Awareness*
- *Anticipation – it's different*
- *Observation skills*
- *Practical skills*

The behaviour and actions of all riders are as individual as a fingerprint. Use of the Competence Fingerprint will help you to determine, as a Trainer, the issues you have observed and how you wish to address and discuss those issues with your student.

For both initial assessment and all subsequent development and training, any aspect of their riding can be categorised into one of these headings:

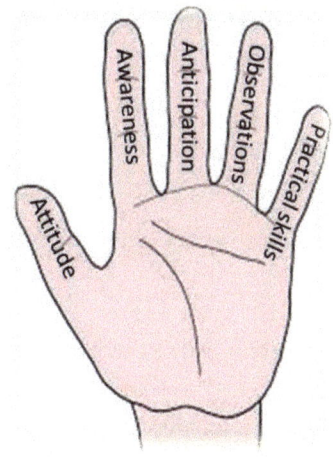

- Attitude
- Awareness
- Anticipation
- Observation Skills
- Practical Skills

The Competence Fingerprint is a deliberately simplistic short hand aid to remembering and categorising the actions and behaviours you observe in your students as a Trainer. You do not have the luxury of a secretary riding pillion taking notes. You need to be able remain safe in your ride but to also recall, categorise and address the issues you observe. You will be making subconscious associations between your recollections and your fingertips making it easier to provide feedback at the end of the training session.

ATTITUDE

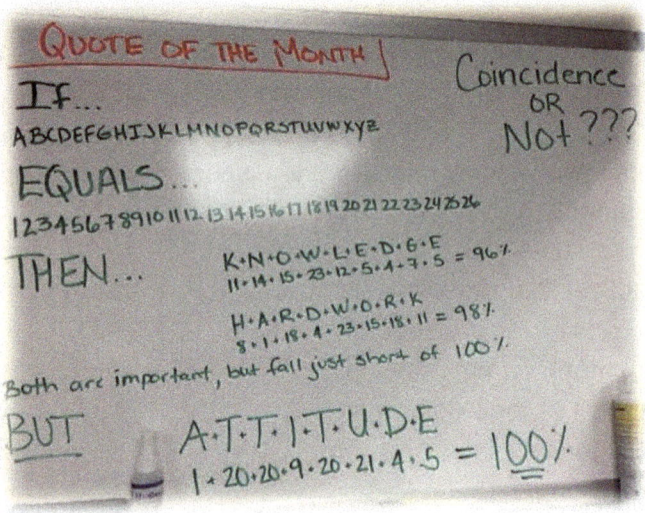

This is the thumb which lets the fingers grip.

With the wrong (negative) attitude, nothing else will work effectively and the student will be a hazard to himself, you and other road users.

As a Trainer, it is vitally important that you recognise that you will need to build relationships with your students. You need your students to have a positive attitude at all times. Any negativity, clash of personalities or unresolved differences of opinion will affect the mood and temperament of those involved and that, of course, also includes you. In situations like this, training will become difficult, if not impossible to undertake. In extreme cases, this may require the current and/or future training sessions to be postponed or even cancelled.

Something that cannot be overlooked is the reality that the majority of your training will take place on open roads and weather will affect the mood of both you and your students. Being cold and wet is not fun and training should be fun. Being adequately kitted out with cold and wet weather equipment goes a long way to maintaining the feel good factor. We have cancelled many training sessions on the grounds of safety due to weather conditions.

In Cyprus, when it rains it is torrential and can be accompanied with strong winds. The general design of the roads, without gutters and drains, means surface water does not readily flow away and can be a major hazard. At the other extreme, training sessions are suspended for the month of August when the heat and humidity is unbearable and it is not unusual for temperatures to reach 40°C!

The terminology "Road Rage" and the interactions between road users, do not really need any explanation to realise the negativity and sometimes danger it brings onto the road and to your personal safety.

On the road we advocate and train to improve anticipation. It will help you if you consider, in advance, how you would deal with a situation were you ever to witness a student do something that provokes a road rage incident. You should also consider your response to a student who reacts to provocation with retaliation aimed at the road user who upset them. If you ensure that your students always respect other road users such events are unlikely to happen.

It is important to watch how the student behaves or reacts to the movement or presence of other road users. Is the student relaxed, comfortable, nervous, aggressive, tense, over cautious, appears tired or feeling unwell?

What would you like to see from a student? We would suggest someone who is courteous, showing consideration to other road users, is alert and does not abuse the bike they are riding. Above all, you want someone who you would feel comfortable and safe to ride with.

At the opposite end of the scale, would you want to be with someone who is aggressive verbally, gesticulates, uses their bike to intimidate other road users, is impatient, wants to "police" other road users or has succumbed to the "red mist", during which time he or she is oblivious to the risks they expose themselves to? You would feel unsafe, nervous and at the least uncomfortable about their behaviour. Would you ride with them?

As Trainers, we know we would prefer someone with lower proficiency and good attitude than the reverse. A bad attitude is the much more difficult to address.

Awareness and Anticipation

You will have to confirm your students' abilities by analysing how they implement IPSGA. Reinforce your assessment with frequent questions and answers at appropriate briefings, de-briefings and breaks. When appropriate, provide plenty of examples which you have seen on the road as a basis for analysis and discussion.

Awareness is the state, or condition, of having identified and recognised a situation or set of circumstances. Anticipation is processing that information to predict a set of possible outcomes which you, as a rider (student or Trainer), can take action on to maintain your safety and that of other road users. If you are aware of the ball in the road, do you anticipate the following child and/or the stopping car, then the opening door?

It is always good to find out from a student what they understand the words "awareness" and "anticipation" actually mean. It is quite common that the answer you will get is that they are the same or similar. Talk it through with them and clear up any ambiguity, so they have a clear understanding of what you will be talking about. Ask the student to give you some examples of awareness as a biker. Prepare them for the next training session with you by asking them to give you an example of awareness and anticipation. Have them explain something that worked for them on their ride to meet up with you. Furthermore, there is nothing wrong with always making this request each time you meet. Examples of awareness and anticipation are boundless.

Think of the brain as being a library in which every new experience of awareness and anticipation is filed under "rider experience".

Examples of **poor** awareness would be: not recognising hazards, late recognition of hazards, looking at, but not seeing, hazards or not prioritising hazards appropriately for action.

Examples of **good** awareness would be: being able to clearly identify hazards, recognising them early enough so as not to be caught unawares and to correctly prioritise them.

You need to confirm the level of a student's anticipation skill and ability, in much the same way as you will do for their awareness. You should observe and analyse how they implement IPSGA to ascertain their skill level. Reinforce your assessment with frequent questions and answers. When you stop to discuss the ride, if appropriate, provide plenty of examples of the "what ifs" from what you have seen and what you were then anticipating at the time.

Examples of **poor** anticipation would be: being caught out by the movement of other road users, not expecting the unexpected, incorrectly assessing the situation they are in and what potentially could happen.

Examples of **good** anticipation would be: not being caught out, recognising the potential for and being ready to deal with, "something" that has yet to happen. Typically this would be demonstrated by changes in your student's position, speed and/or gear selection under IPSGA.

Awareness	Anticipation
The brow of the hill is seen…	What is over the other side? Anything could be on the other side
There is extensive surface water…	How deep is the water? Is there a hole in the road? What is my route through the water? Imagine what would happen if the water is ridden into at too fast a speed

On the road give examples, over the radio, of your own thinking to demonstrate what you are aware of and what you anticipate it might mean. This direct mentoring is invaluable to your students.

Sometimes you must state the obvious. What is obvious to you may not be to your student, depending on their experience. State the less obvious examples you believe your student would benefit from, but also keep on stating the obvious to reinforce the message that nothing is being overlooked. Remember to communicate this early enough and in as few words as possible, to be of value and to prioritise hazards. Sometimes it will not be possible to talk about every hazard, you will have seen them, but you just will not have had the time to point them out before they are behind you.

Some frequent useful examples:-

> "Petrol station left, vehicles in and out".
> "Car at junction left, may pull out, check wheels for movement"
> "Vehicles have body language, check oncoming vehicle, bonnet dipping, it could turn right across your path"
> "Smell of freshly cut undergrowth, works vehicles and men may be around the bend".
> "Delivery truck just pulled up left, if brake lights go out, be ready for door opening"

On the move staccato diction is not only acceptable but essential to speedy comms…

THE STUDENT'S BIKE CAN SPEAK TO THE TRAINER...

 Your student's use of the horn can tell you about their anticipation. As a practical exercise, take time to talk to your students about the use of the horn. It is the voice of the bike. You may be surprised at how many riders are reluctant to use it! You may also witness them use it when it is too late to be effective. The student is being reactive and not proactive and missed the opportunity to sound the horn a moment earlier to maximise its effect. Increased levels of awareness and anticipation will be confirmed by correct use of the horn, such as when a student becomes aware of and anticipates the movement of another road user, before their position increases the risk to your student and use of the horn prevents the car from pulling out in front of them. The horn has been used for what it was intended and at the right time.

It also helps to know where the horn button is. BMW riders (dependant on model of bike) will confirm that the position of the horn button on the left handlebar can result in a rider pressing the turn left signal instead! The way we overcame this difficulty was to keep on practicing sounding the horn. We must reassure you that we chose our moments to do this. What this did was to train our left thumbs to locate the horn every time. We still do this exercise and it has been of immense value to us, when we have had reason to use it. No more fumbling for the horn and not being able to use it, or signalling left and giving out false information. It is safer too.

Without radio communication, feedback on the move will be impossible. You will have to rely on your memory, as well as your observation skills and then discuss any incidents that have arisen when you stop. This review discussion is essential for you to be able to ascertain what the student was aware or unaware of and if the student was prepared to react to the hazard being discussed.

When awareness and anticipation is inadequate, it can hurt...a lot. As a police officer one of the authors attended a rider only crash where the rider had been practising "making progress" through bends. He had been focused on his position, speed and lean of his bike. He came unstuck when he put his right knee down, as he thought this was the best way to ride a bend. He seemed unaware of and did not anticipate the consequences of being on a public road, rather than the track. Cat's eyes are solid, heavy and firmly secured in the road surface. So when his right kneecap hit a cat's eye the result was the painful removal of said kneecap! Big Ouch!

OBSERVATIONS

Observation is fundamental to being able to ride safely for yourself and other road users. As a Trainer, you must observe your student's actions and behaviour, to identify where his or her lack of observation skill is contributing negatively to their development as an advanced rider.

You should ensure your student recognises all traffic signs and understands what they mean.

To be a master of time, speed and distance, observation is the key. It enables information to be assimilated, prioritised and processed such that the rider can follow the IPSGA system effectively AND efficiently.

It is not unusual to find riders' observation techniques let them down dramatically at the Information phase:

- **They look but do not see**
- **See but are not aware**
- **Aware but do not anticipate**
- **Anticipate but do not prepare**

FORWARD OBSERVATIONS

The scanning technique is paramount to providing the time to implement IPSGA. Continually encourage your student to keep their vision lifted up and look to infinity.

They should scan to get an early view of the road ahead, which may be to one side or the other and even above or below their current position.

This helps to identify the road layout and hazards ahead and to prioritise them for the "Information" phase of riding to the System.

Encourage your student to look for information in unlikely places and to be flexible with their positioning to get the best possible view. A lot of the road ahead and therefore the hazards can be seen by looking down the left, right, under and over and even through the vehicles and other objects in front and around them.

Some examples of looking through objects would be vehicle windows and trees and bushes.

Scan through the trees and undergrowth – what do you see? What will it mean to your safety?

The latter provides an increased view when the foliage has thinned or dropped as the seasons change. But the road surface may be worse!

Get them to take advantage of reflections on windows of buildings and body panels of vehicles etc. – they will be able to see around corners.

Radio communications are invaluable to give examples of how far ahead and where the Trainer is looking for information which can be announced to the student. State the obvious as it significantly helps the students to assess their own skill. It highlights the importance of the need to look as far ahead as possible and in circumstances they are unaccustomed to. They will also appreciate how much is seen in so short a time, all of it relevant to the safety of the ride. A positive aspect of this technique is that the student will be pleased with their performance when your comments accurately reflect what they are seeing too.

IDENTIFYING RIDERS LEVEL OF OBSERVATION

Now all you have to do is to identify any riding behaviour that highlights a shortfall in good observation techniques. Here are some examples:

- Staring, also applicable to mirror use, is a major distraction from awareness and anticipation for the road ahead. It is the opposite of scanning. A rider's hands will follow their eyes and the rider will steer towards what they are looking at; for example, looking at oncoming vehicles and moving towards the centre of the road.

- Looking, but not seeing; where the student is approaching a junction and does not recognise opportunities to emerge safely and progressively, so the student stops to make sure it is safe looking both ways before moving off. Look for signs of staring too long in one direction, or both, rather than short rhythmic observations to absorb lots of information from scanning the whole scene correctly. Their vision may be short and not looking far enough to assess opportunities for them to emerge from the junction. At roundabouts, check that the student does not fixate on any vehicle in front of which they intend to pull out. **The student must look to where they want to go**. Having entered the roundabout, check that the student does not make another observation to the right, as there cannot be another vehicle once they have identified their gap. It is unnecessary, will slow down their progress and is putting focus behind/right when it should be in the direction of travel.

- Following, or stopping too close to the vehicle in front. The student's vision will be blocked and their scanning technique will therefore not be effective. The bigger the vehicle, the bigger the scanning obstruction.

- Speeding... if the signs are not recognized, or the student's reaction is delayed... do not be tempted to follow at the same speed just to see when the student will react. You are potentially compromising your own driving licence. Use your radio to tell the student what the speed limit is. If the student slowed down when you told them to, but you did not tell the student what the speed limit was, they could end up riding too fast or too slow.

- Another consideration is riding within the speed limit, but too fast for the conditions. A good example of this is riding past a school when the children are leaving it. The limit may be 30mph (50kph), but the road is congested with parked cars, doors are being opened and children and parents are walking and running between vehicles. The hazards are numerous, so the student's speed should reflect that and be slow enough to stop safely if required.

- Tunnel vision, not using peripheral vision or moving the head side to side to see more than is directly in front of them. Very characteristic of the rider who tailgates the vehicle in front. Do you fixate on the car ahead?

Or see the whole picture and multitude of other hazards – speed limit, parked vehicles, speed table, pedestrian crossing, obscured vehicle emerging from junction on left?

- Your student overshoots a give way line or stop line before coming to a stop. What were they focused on and where were they looking? How did they miss the line in front of them? They may have had every intention of stopping before it, but did not slow down sufficiently enough to stop in time. It is also quite possible that a student may deliberately edge ahead of vehicles at a stop line controlled by traffic lights to be first away and to get a better view. This behaviour must be addressed as the correct place to be is behind the line.

- Cutting a right hand corner generally, from a major to minor road, when vision is restricted into the new road, with the obvious risk that some other road user coming the other way may not be seen, forcing subsequent avoiding action.

- Moving out late to pass parked vehicles, other obstructions or metal covers on the road surface. It looks like the rider is swerving, more than gently steering around the hazard and it may be compounded by swerving back after the hazard has been passed. To overcome this style of riding, get your student to recognise the hazard earlier and glide out to pass it with very little steering, to pass parallel to the hazard at a safe distance. It is also good to discuss a situation where a student sees a hazard on the road surface ahead and has a choice of either going to the left or right of it. Which way do they go? By scanning and recognising all the hazards, an informed decision can be made. For example, a student needs to avoid a pothole in his line of travel past parked cars. There are oncoming vehicles. If the student steers left, he/she will get close to the parked cars and there is the danger of a door being opened. That is, if it is occupied. A student can check this by effective scanning. A student can consider going to the right of the pothole if they adjust their speed to pass the hazard in a safe gap in the oncoming traffic flow. A sure sign that a student has not recognised, or thought through a route past the pothole, is when you see them ride through it!

- A student may find themselves in a position of danger if they commit to an overtake and have not scanned ahead of the vehicle they intend to overtake. For example, they have passed a road warning sign that indicates there is a road junction ahead and the overtake is happening alongside the junction. The potential for disaster is very obvious and had they seen the sign, they would have held back.

- A student is turning right from a major road to a minor road and has to stop due to the presence and movement of vehicles approaching from the opposite direction. When there is a gap in the traffic, the student moves off and swan-necks the junction because they were too far forward for the turn when they stopped. Get your student to recognise that, if they need to stop, hold back from their point of turn by about 2 metres so that they turn into the road they are on the correct course.

REARWARD OBSERVATIONS

At a convenient briefing, have a short question and answer session with your student to find out what they can see in their mirrors and how they position them for maximum effect. Ensure both mirrors are positioned correctly on your student's bike and your own before you ride, they may have been knocked if you were parked up.

Mirror checks must be co-ordinated with the use of IPSGA. Their frequency of use is dependent on the hazards and early recognition of what may be fast approaching from behind. How long does the "look" take? Generally, a fraction of a second, otherwise it becomes a stare.

Mirrors should definitely be checked when your student is required to alter or change their:

- **course** - moving to the left or right
- **direction** turning left or right or exiting a roundabout
- **speed** - moving off, braking, acceleration, deceleration and stopping

Blind spots

The student should be flexible and supple in the riding seat and be aware of blind spots.   Not just over their shoulders, but what is ahead of them hidden by trees, street furniture, parked vehicles etc.

Checking of blind spots before moving off, even in a traffic queue, is vital for the safety of the student and other road users.   There is many a delay between the intended move off and the actual go! The habit of making an additional check behind when moving away, even when parallel to the kerb, gives extra assurance that it is still safe to do so.

Lifesavers are quick scans over either one or both shoulders, whilst maintaining road position, to check blind spots for the movement of other road users before changing course or direction.   This is particularly important when moving from one lane to another.   Never let your student forget to do them.   It will save their life one day!

A lifesaver is the momentary turning of the head, using neck movement only, for a fraction of a second. The torso should not be twisted, as this movement will cause your student to steer in the direction of the shoulder they are checking over. Too long and the view to the front is sacrificed.   Too short and something might be missed.   It is not a look upwards or down to the road surface. It is a check of the blind spots.

Faults to rectify:

- no or infrequent use of mirrors
- uncoordinated mirror checks
- no or missed lifesavers checks
- lifesavers too early or too late
- lifesavers too long or too short

PRACTICAL SKILLS

- *Gloved hands*
- *Steering – counter steering*
- *Identifying and correcting bad habits*
- *Signals and gestures*
- *Throttle, clutch and gears*
- *Use of brakes*

For the purpose of the "Fingerprint", it is easy to recall all matters relating to machine control under this heading. The riding of the machine should be second nature for any would be advanced rider, so that their attention is directed to the planning and execution of their ride. For example, maintaining balance and slow speed momentum, whilst checking for a gap in the traffic to facilitate an easy emerge onto a busy main road, takes an enormous amount of skill. A rider should not have to concern him/herself with brakes, clutch and fine throttle control as well.

Your role is to help the student achieve this Zen like state.

It is best for any rider to be relaxed and comfortable on their rides. It is amazing how many riders choose a bike for its looks and performance and do not take into account how comfortable they will be for the rides they want to do, or their body size. Ask any sports bike rider what it is like after a long ride and they will complain of sore wrists, neck, back, legs and feet. They are not the most comfortable of machines and if the rider is not comfortable, they certainly will not be relaxed and alert in their ride. The trade-off for riding a sports bike on a long journey should be to take frequent breaks and stretch out, rather than just stopping for refuelling.

As a Trainer, you will discover that the practical knowledge and skills of the riders you meet will vary dramatically, from extremely proficient, to people that drive and don't ride their bike. Just like other aspects of training, a question and answer session on how a bike is ridden, will provide you with a picture of what to expect from a student. Also, stating the obvious keeps the interaction between you and the student alive, confirms you "know your stuff" and reinforces their own knowledge.

Now, let's look at how the hands and feet perform to keep the bike moving and how the controls are best used for maximum effect. And yes, to some of you, we will be stating the obvious in the best possible way.

HANDS

There is a wide choice of gloves for riders to suit their needs and budget. However, irrespective of choice, the thickness of gloves worn will affect the feedback to rider's hands. Gloves that are too tight will restrict movement of hands and fingers and gloves that are too loose can slip on the brake and clutch levers. So it is important to choose a pair that fits correctly.

STEERING

A good steering technique only requires a light but firm grip of the handlebars and if riding over a rough surface or uneven road, a rider should be ready to tighten the grip slightly. It is not a white knuckle ride, irrespective of the speed being ridden at. If the hands are tense, then the arms and shoulders of the rider will tense up too. A rider should be relaxed, with the arms slightly bent, in order to exercise full control of their machine.

COUNTER STEERING

Counter steering is used whenever a rider needs to change direction. This applies to basic cornering manoeuvres, as well as evasive manoeuvres, such as swerving. It is also important to be able to counter steer effectively when a corner suddenly tightens more than expected, or when committed to a turn into a bend and the approach speed is too fast.

It is the most effective way to get a motorcycle to go from being upright to a leaning position.

Press on the right handlebar to lean to the right and press on the left handlebar to lean to the left. By applying forward pressure onto either the left or right handlebar in the direction a rider wants to turn, the bike will fall into a lean. The more pressure the further the lean and tighter the turn.

To Go Left · To Go Right

Push on Left Bar · Push on Right Bar

Moves Contact Patch to Right of C of G · Moves Contact Patch to Left of C of G

IDENTIFYING BAD HABITS

Let's consider some of the most common "bad" habits that riders acquire over the years and which you, as a Trainer, need to rectify:

- One handed steering as a student stretches their arm, or rests their hand on their hip to pose for effect as they ride. We've seen many riders assume this position at fast speeds in bends and panic set in when they need to get their hand back on the handlebar. The forward thrust of the arm and impact of the hand on the handlebar can introduce unexpected counter steer and surprise the student even more.

- No hands on the handlebars. Now there really is no excuse for this one, but you will still see it. It might be for a stretch or just posing but, seriously, a student is not in control of their bike at all in this situation and it will take at least one second to get their hands back onto the handlebar to regain control when needed.

- There will be times when one handed steering can be thought through and opted for. It will only take a moment. Some examples are when giving hand signals, wiping a visor clear of rain or raising it for ventilation. However, the moment should be chosen wisely. It would be unwise to wipe a visor on approach to a hazard. The priority must be the hazard and there is a need to be in full control as it is approached.

INDICATING

Use of indicators; generally the base of the hands will stay in contact with the handlebar and a thumb will be used to turn on and off the indicators. Switch gear varies with different manufacturers of bikes. Generally, the cancel button can be incorporated with the turn signal switch or separate from it. A student should familiarise themselves as to where they are and how the switches work. Even if a student knows where the switch is, the way it is designed to operate can still cause difficulty. The was an occasion when riding with a student on a Triumph, on which, to signal, he pushed a switch either left or right. To cancel the signal, the switch needed to be pushed in. What actually happened is that his thumb slid diagonally across the switch, which did not push it in far enough, so the signal remained on. He had to be radioed frequently to cancel it. He would look down to make sure it had cancelled, when he should have been looking where he intended to go.

After discussion with the student, he modified his thumb position and practiced the movement until he perfected a technique which, he was sure, cancelled the signal without the need for him to visually check this action.

It is important that students are confident in the use of signals and that they are used and cancelled as intended. A signal given when not intended or not cancelled is a serious risk to the health of a rider if another road user acts on what they see.

WHETHER IT IS NOBLER TO USE INDICATORS?

To use, or not to use, indicators to good effect as an advanced rider is something which has been widely debated because signalling should not be automatically incorporated into a ride **if** there is no likelihood of another road user benefit from it. This is where the consideration of whether or not to use indicators differs greatly from when learning to ride. So what does the word "if" mean in this context? The decision must be based on what is seen, what the rider is aware of and what the rider is anticipating – what can't be seen.

This topic, just like the rest of your time spent training riders, must be kept simple. We believe your students should have no doubt that the use of a signal should be given if it would be of benefit to another road user. Let a student make their own decision based on what they can see, what they can't see and what they can reasonably anticipate happening all around them. This continually improves their scanning technique, so if they choose not to signal, they will be confident they made the right decision. Get ready to answer the question as to whether or not a dog is a road user. I am sure you will deal with this admirably when the time comes but be ready when they then ask you, "Is it the same for guide dogs?"

The decision as to whether or not to give a signal rests with the student. It is given full consideration by a rider in the first stage of IPSGA – INFORMATION. This has three phases, take, use and give. A signal is giving information. The rider can then apply themselves to the remaining stages of the System. But let's consider the reality of what actually needs to be considered by the rider.

When IPSGA is used, it should include consideration for the appropriate time of giving a signal whilst using the System. In fact the Information stage may be too early for a signal to be given. Flexibility is the answer to giving a signal or not. For example, a student may be riding towards a junction and depending on the distance away from it, may actually be at the Speed stage of the System before a signal is given. On the other hand, if a signal is not given, there will be a point of no return. After which, to give a signal may detract from the concentration and safety of the student, whilst being too late to benefit another road user. Our advice is, if in doubt, give a signal. Others, we know, may disagree!

Indeed, there will be moments when your student gives a signal and you do not and vice versa. Such is the difference in decisions because of the small gap in the time, speed and distance between you and your student.

There will be plenty of opportunities to ask a student why they did, or why they didn't give a signal. Remember, it is their decision making process you are talking about and you will be wanting to hear a rational explanation of their thought processes, rather than the signal having been given automatically with no thought at all.

With your input, your student's decision making as to when or when not to signal, can be left to them. Some guidance may be needed when the available time, speed and distance has resulted in a signal being given too late, too early or not co-ordinated well with their progress on the road. You will have ample opportunities to feedback, discuss and reflect on the use of indicators and the message that was given out.

Generally, when turning right at a mini-roundabout, a signal should be given unless there is no need to do so. When exiting a mini-roundabout, the priority for the student must be to steer their bike. Due to the relatively slow speed and the body language of the bike, the need to signal left to exit the mini roundabout need not be activated, unless the student chooses to do so and their steering is not affected by this action.

ARM SIGNALS

Reinforcing a signal can be very effective to raise the awareness of other road users of a rider's intention or if a bulb fails on the bike, for example the brake light. We have used the slowing down signal many times on the approach to a pedestrian crossing to re-enforce the brake light. It is also good to think about giving a left turn arm signal when exiting a roundabout if you have any doubt about the movement of other road users behind you, even though you will have done a lifesaver.

Fortunately, bulb failures are not as common as they used to be but it does stress the importance of doing the POWERED check routinely to find any such defects before riding.

One of the authors was riding with a student some time ago when his brake bulb failed. The student was radioed to stop. He did not have a spare bulb, so it was suggested it was an opportunity for him to give slowing down arm signals, to which he answered, "How do I do that?" Having shown him what to do and what to avoid, before riding off, he was asked to show arm signals for turning right and left. This he also asked to be demonstrated. Back to stating and showing what could be perceived to be the obvious: if he had not been asked to see his arm signals for turning, it could have been assumed, wrongly, that he knew how to do them.

COURTESY GESTURE

Another road user can make a rider's day by being courteous and vice versa. It may be the waving of a hand or the flashing of headlights. When acknowledged, it gives a feeling of wellbeing to both the person who gave way and the person taking advantage.

A word of caution though, before a rider or in this case your student reacts to the "invite" without appropriate care and full all round observations, as they could be riding into danger.

It is good to take advantage of what the other road user wishes to let you do, so long as it is safe to do so. Note, there is but an instant to process your thoughts and act before the opportunity is lost. Other road users can be very impatient and any protracted delay may be interpreted as you will not go, even by the person who has made the offer. Generally, the quickest and safest way to acknowledge the courtesy shown is a nod of the head in their direction.

What if your student decides to be courteous? There will be times when common sense suggests it and it is safe to allow another road user precedence. Why not? Just coming to a stop may be insufficient for the other road user to respond, except, of course, at a pedestrian crossing. So, having made the decision to allow another road user priority, your student will need to do something to let the other person know he has been given precedence. In situations like this, your student has to accept responsibility for their actions and be "absolutely bomb proof", that he is not inviting the other person into danger. If the student has stopped and is in gear, they cannot use their left arm or hand as the clutch lever is being held in. The two considerations are, a brief wave of the right hand or a nod of the head from side to side, because without some gesture, the other person will not have a clue what to do. Our preference is the latter, the head movement, whilst we remain in full control of our bikes.

We have not mentioned flashing the headlight, as the correct use is exclusively as a warning. We doubt if the other road user is actually focused on a headlight anyway. The rider is in full view to the other person and their vision is naturally directed towards the upper body and head of a rider for any visible sign that they can now go.

A further word of caution is needed for riders, about how other road users interpret headlamp flashing as a courtesy gesture. The majority of bikes now run with the headlight on. If a rider is on a main road, which is undulating and bumpy, **to a motorist waiting to emerge from a side road, looking at the headlight it will appear that they have been flashed at.** They may pull out. So be aware and anticipate that this could happen. One day it will and you must prepare your student for such an eventuality.

When observing the actions of your student and you hear yourself thinking "He could have given way there". You are probably right. What was the reason for not helping another road user who was experiencing difficulty and it was perfectly safe to do so? If it is a case of "I couldn't be bothered" or "I had right of way anyway", then perhaps the appropriate amount of consideration for others was not given? Turn it back onto the student and ask them if the situation had been reversed, would they have appreciated the offer of help. We very much doubt that they will say "No".

You may also witness your student react immediately to an offer to go first and nothing untoward happens. However, you also doubt that effective mirror checks and observations were undertaken. Quite possibly your student also fails to acknowledge the kind gesture made towards them. That lack of acknowledgement is an easy way to upset or annoy another road user, who may no longer show respect towards bikers. We know this can happen because many drivers, over the years, have made some unsavoury and uncomplimentary remarks to us about rider attitudes.

You must not ignore such events but talk them through with the student, reinforcing the "what ifs" that should have been considered first. It only takes a moment to do this but, if ignored, it only takes another moment for the student to find themself horizontal and in need of an ambulance. Is it worth it?

THROTTLE

Discuss with your student how they use the throttle under acceleration and observe what they do on their rides. Do they understand the rev range and road speed available to them in each gear? We mention this because a significant number of riders do not fully appreciate how increased revs can improve road holding, stability and performance. It often helps a student to experience how their bike performs in different gears, using increased revs, to make them a more competent rider.

Do they understand the concept of "rolling on" and "rolling off" the throttle? Under acceleration the throttle is twisted gently to keep the front wheel firmly in contact with the road surface and not to transfer too much weight from front to rear. Too much throttle applied too quickly carries the risk of raising the front wheel off the ground. Many riders like to do this, but public roads are not the place for such practice as the risks associated with it, not just for the rider, but also for other road users, are totally unacceptable.

The throttle is also a very effective tool to help the slowing down of a bike. The first stage of braking is actually rolling off the throttle. The higher the revs and the lower the gear, the bigger the effect of engine braking, felt through the seat of the pants. A very good exercise to undertake with your student is to get them to ride using the throttle and gears only to control their speed. This is called acceleration sense and it is very effective.

Another effective way to use the throttle is when changing down through the gears. As a rider goes down a gear, the engine revs increase. Blipping the throttle quickly, when the clutch lever is pulled in, momentarily increases the engine revs to nearly match the new gear. Ideally, when this skill is perfected, the revs will exactly match the road speed of the bike for a smooth downward gear change.

Once your student has mastered acceleration sense, they will fully appreciate the importance of it, especially for control of speed and stability when cornering and when riding downhill. A student will be able to ride comfortably downhill, under power, when their choice of gear and engine revs counteracts the force of gravity. This is a much more comfortable experience than the floaty, unsettling feeling, which may cause the rider to brake, even in a bend. Doing so incorrectly may give them a much bigger problem to deal with!

Traits which might need your attention as Trainer could be, little or no "acceleration sense", with the student constantly showing signs of being either on or off the throttle, travelling too quickly or too slowly for the conditions, forcing you to adjust your speed and following distance. You would also observe jerky acceleration/deceleration and with harsh or insufficient use of the brakes through the body language of the rider, who will be pitched forward or backwards accordingly.

FRONT BRAKE

Is the student smooth and progressive in the application of the front brake? Has he or she allowed sufficient time to cover, gently squeeze and then progressively increase brake pressure through their observation of the road conditions and application of IPSGA? The front brake provides the most powerful stopping on a motorcycle and on most modern machines can, in the  absence of ABS (Anti-lock Brake System), easily lock the front wheel. In less than expert hands, this would inevitably result in a loss of control and a crash. Applying too much pressure to the front brake will cause the front suspension to compress, will put a large down force on the student's arms, which he must resist to maintain forward vision and may even lift the rear wheel off the road in what is known as a "stopee" for those prone to showing off!

On public roads, the front brake should only be used to reduce speed rapidly whilst travelling in a straight line. Using it to help the bike turn in for a bend is a skill to perfect under professional training on a closed circuit where medical assistance is available during early practice!

Typically, an advanced rider will use 2, 3 or 4 fingers to give the finesse and delicacy the front brake requires. Use of only one finger is not recommended, as most people will find that they either have insufficient strength or dexterity.

Think back to our objective of being the masters of time, speed and distance. Covering the brake in anticipation that it may be needed saves about one second. This could be the difference between a comfortable, controlled stop and a painful experience!

CLUTCH

The clutch is designed to be used momentarily to enable engine rev changes to match road speed and gear selection in a smooth operation, either when moving off from stationary or changing up and down through the gears on the move. The plates in the clutch slip against one another to provide this smooth synchronisation of gearbox and engine. If it is slipped too frequently, it will heat up and wear out. Letting it in too quickly will be demonstrated by jerky progress on the move or when setting off and the rider will need tuition to help improve his use of it. Sometimes as Trainer, you may observe a student pull in the clutch on the move without changing gear. The rider is then coasting and his machine is not then properly under control. Why was this done?

Usually it means IPSGA has not been properly implemented. Often this will be in a left or right turn or it may be using the clutch too early when coming to a stop. As Trainer, you must try to find out why in order to identify the root causes and address them. It will almost always be related to time or lack of it, in which the rider's preparations should have been completed. An easy cure for the left and right turn problem is to ensure the student aims to complete his work, e. g. downward gear changes, at least one car length before the actual turn. This will ensure that the clutch is fully engaged and the rider is ready to proceed.

ANCILLARY CONTROLS

As Trainer, you are concerned to ensure that your student knows where the controls are instinctively, without looking and knows when to use them. Instinctive use comes only with frequent practice which creates "muscle memory". Fingers and thumbs react to mental intentions and not only conscious thought. The horn is a particularly pertinent example because its use forecasts the presence of the bike to others but only if used early enough. Fumble for the button and it will be too late. You cannot be a Zen Master and fumble. To be a Zen Master, practice. Apply the horn time after time when no one can hear it, just to become familiar with its use. Do the same with indicators and hazard warnings, music centres, all that your bike is equipped with.

FEET

The objective is to synchronise hand (clutch and throttle) and foot (gear lever) coordination to effect smooth gear changing up and down the box and includes block gear changes (one or more gears missed out without being engaged). The student should know which gear he is selecting and what his machine's performance **will be** in that gear. Many high performance machines are capable of speeds which are multiples of the national speed limits.

Restraint may be one of the most important aspects of a rider's development to become an advanced rider. Like hot chilli paste – use sparingly and wisely!

Almost any modern machine of 400cc or more is capable of speeds well in excess of the national speed limits, even in the lower gears. Economy is provided by using the higher gears and lower revs.

Eyes should go to infinity and beyond with your scanning but test your machine's performance on a closed circuit if you feel such need for speed!

REAR BRAKE

Speaking as someone who came late to the advantages of rear brake use, it was a complete revelation. Until the 70s, rear brakes were useless and so were many front ones: then Honda introduced the disc brake on the CB750 in 1969. It was like landing on the moon.

BUT...

Use the rear brake in addition to engine braking and you may never need the front until you decide to go quickly on the open road. Even there, the rear brake comes into its own by enabling safe speed reduction when you do not properly read the bend or you just want to set the bike up before the bend. It provides reassurance that you can still lose a little more speed, even in a bend, if applied gently. In a double apex bend, you may find you need to adjust your speed further for the second apex until the limit point moves. (See Bends below)

On occasion, the road design will compel use of brakes to bring the machine to a complete stop, even in a bend. Use the rear brake to do so.

During slow speed manoeuvres (see below), a little rear brake pressure helps to more easily balance throttle and clutch, giving smoother control of the bike.

The application sequence should be i) cover, ii) gently press the lever, then iii) increase pressure as needed, in a similar manner to that used with the front brake. Smooth and stable is the aim.

Some manufacturers have introduced linked brakes in conjunction with ABS. Apply either front or rear brake and the machine also applies some braking to the other wheel.

ZEN - PHYSICS OF MOTORCYCLES

- *Motorcycle stability*
- *Engine arrangement*
- *Friction – tyre grip*
- *Throttle effects*
- *Brake effects*
- *Straight lines & bends*

An old joke suggests that if one more of the aeroplane's engines fail "We'll be up here all day…"

Well, motorbikes have a lot more in common with aircraft than boats, which are just dead in the water if the engine fails. They just sit there. Bikes might not fall out of the sky but unless they are moving, they fall over. They are only dynamically stable on just two wheels. Stationary they need a stand to prop them up.

Just like an aircraft, which requires a minimum airspeed to become and remain dynamically stable, all the motorcycle controls have secondary effects which you must understand to become a Zen Master. The effects also depend on speed, engine revs and attitude. Not your attitude, that of the bike, although your attitude also matters.

BASIC STABILITY

Fortunately the laws of physics and specifically those relating to gyroscopic effects mean that the two gyroscopes fitted to a bike: the wheels, which help keep the bike upright from very low speeds. If the bike falls one way or the other the gyroscopic effect is to turn the wheels into the direction of fall. Obviously the back wheel cannot turn but it would if it could. Hold that thought for later.

So the gyroscopic effect turns the front wheel, to move the base (the wheel base) back under the centre of gravity to arrest the fall. Is the force with you or what…?

Similarly, if you want to turn, initially you have to steer in the opposite direction to the way you want to go. This is counter steering and what helps is the gyroscopic effect once more: for example, if you initiate a counter steering action to the left (pull on the left bar and push on the right) the gyroscopic effect pushes the bike to fall to the right. This is in addition to the fact that steering left puts the base to the left of the centre of gravity so that gravity wants to pull the bike over to the right.

If you doubt this watch what happens to a lone bicycle wheel rolled along the road. As it starts to fall to one side it rotates to that side and ends up in a faster and faster spiral until it sits spinning on its hub.

You might also now realise why as a child learning to ride a tricycle is exactly the wrong way to learn to ride a bicycle…because you don't learn to initiate turns by moving the bars the opposite way. If you doubt this try riding a push bike using only strings connected to the handlebars and allowing only one to be taught at a time. As you cannot push a string you soon figure out what is happening!

ENGINE ORIENTATION

The rotating parts of the engine constitute another gyroscope and the higher the revs the bigger the effect. If the engine axis is across the bike (a typical in-line four, twin or triple) it provides another stabilising effect like the wheels, making the bike harder to turn.

If the engine axis is in-line with the frame (a typical horizontally opposed twin) this effect will not be so noticeable...

But engines provide power or more specifically the torque to propel the bike. The reaction to the torque applied at the wheel and road interface is on the engine mountings into the frame. If it is mounted across the frame the reaction ends up being taken to the contact patches of the tyres, front and back, and causes a pitching motion. The direction of pitch depends on the engine rotation direction and whether it is applying torque for acceleration or retardation through engine braking.

If the engine axis is in-line, like an R Series BMW, then just blipping the throttle, whilst stationary and feet down, gives a noticeable reaction that is felt by your feet! On the move this is a side force at the contact patches of the tyres, over and above anything being asked of them for acceleration, braking or cornering forces.

Why does this matter?

Ordinarily it does not. But, near the limit for tyre grip it does or it might do. If you were riding on ice you would definitely notice!

FRICTION

Friction is a very fair minded attribute of tyre rubber and its contact with the road. Although tyres can be designed to have clever bracing structures internally to react to acceleration, deceleration and side forces, the rubber tends to be homogenous (uniform in all directions). For a given contact force it will provide a certain lateral friction force in the plane of the road surface.

The fair minded part is that the tyre doesn't care how you arrive at the total friction force. You can have any combination of cornering forces and acceleration or deceleration forces. But the limit is the limit. Less cornering force and you can have more acceleration...or deceleration. More and you cannot.

This is critical. This is the edge. You can keep away from it, get very close, be on it but once you are over it is over...or may be.

THROTTLE

The obvious effect of opening the throttle is to increase engine revs, increase torque at the back wheel, cause the bike to accelerate and thus transfer weight from the front to the back wheel, increasing the back wheel's ability to deliver traction because friction between tyre and road is proportional to the weight on the tyre.

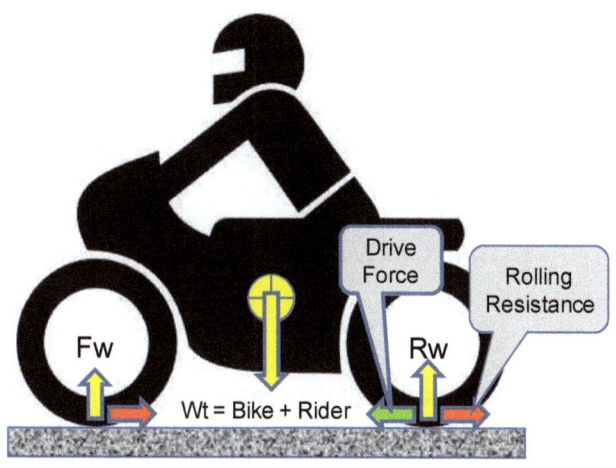

The weight (Wt) of bike and rider acts through the combined centre of gravity and is balanced by the vertical forces from the road (Fw) at the front wheel and (Rw) rear wheel. Usually the bike is slightly front wheel heavy before the rider is added.

If you accelerate hard you may be able to "pull a wheelie" if the bike has enough torque...not power. As the front wheel lifts, all the weight must be carried by the rear wheel. The distance between the back wheel contact patch and centre of gravity multiplied by the moment arm will then balance the torque delivered to the rear wheel. The torque equals the force at the contact patch (providing the acceleration)

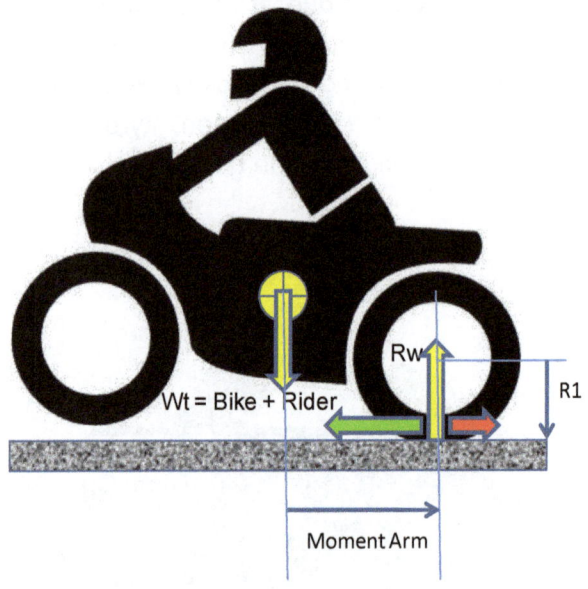

multiplied by the radius of the wheel including tyre.

If the front wheel lifts significantly into the air the torque has to be reduced (by closing the throttle) because the moment arm is reduced as the angle of the bike and rider increases. Maximum acceleration is when the front wheel is just fractionally off the road! More than that is dangerous because of lack of steering and provides no performance gain. An expert demonstrating a stable "wheelie" is not accelerating but travelling at a constant speed with torque, rolling resistance and aerodynamic drag all in perfect balance.

Now consider closing the throttle. Deceleration provides a weight transfer to the front and consequent reduction at the rear. Perhaps only with a large single cylinder engine would the retardation torque of the engine be sufficient to lose traction on a metalled dry road, but on a wet or slippery surface it could very easily do so.

You also need to make sure that your student recognises the need for a small increase in throttle when the bike is leaned over simply to maintain speed.

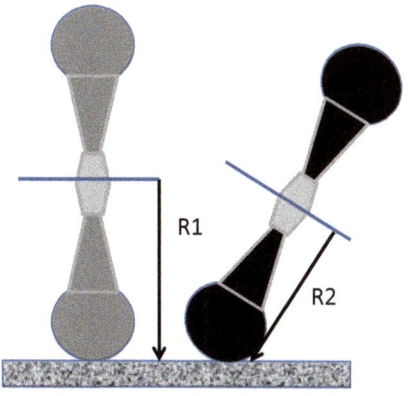

Wheel radius R1 when upright is typically about 30cm (nominal 2ft wheel diameter) whilst leaned over R2 is about 1cm less than R1. That is around a 3% reduction. So to maintain a constant speed around a bend with that amount of lean will require a 3% increase in engine revs. Add this effect to the increased road resistance when executing a bend and without increased throttle the bike will slow down markedly.

BRAKES

Brakes have a similar weight transfer and pitching effect on the bike. The consequence is similar but opposite to throttle. Back braking will fairly easily bring the tyre to its adhesion limit. On the other hand using the front brake puts more weight on the front increasing the available friction force the tyre can deliver. Hence it is perfectly possible, on a good road surface to do a "stoppie" in which the back wheel lifts into the air.

A racer can typically hold the bike for some distance with the rear wheel in the air as he comes to a stop. He may even turn the bike around on the front tyre contact patch. It is the result of physics, practice to develop skill and good road surface and tyres. Unless you can control the conditions the last two will be your downfall.

CLUTCH

Ok, so we know this disconnects the engine and gearbox. So what?

When the clutch lever is squeezed there can be no transmission of engine torque, either acceleration or retardation to the back wheel and nor can there be any torque reaction generated at the tyre contact patches. You just might need to remember this one day...

DYNAMIC STABILITY

You gotta move to get the groove...

So much for the physics, what does it mean?

STRAIGHT LINES

In a straight line you will experience the big effects and that is part of the exhilaration of biking. High "G" forces deliver excitement right up until the point of impact! If you lock up the back wheel under braking you will more or less continue travelling in a straight line. The back end might waggle around a little but unless you make another change you are unlikely to drop the bike. You have time to recognise what is happening and to correct it. A stoppie, whilst generally to be avoided, is unlikely to cause a fall on a dry road in a straight line. The gyroscopic effect is acting in your favour to prevent a fall.

A wheelie is fairly stable if throttle control is finessed. Again the gyroscopic effect tries to keep the bike from falling to one side and steering inputs to a rotating front wheel in the air will apply steering forces as a result of the gyroscopic effect.

BENDS

Bends are a whole different ball game!

On a grippy surface too much throttle will cause the bike to want to move onto a larger radius, go wide which must be countered by increased lean delivered initially by a counter steering action which appears to deliberately take the bike wide. This takes the rider nearer the edge of the road or closer to oncoming traffic depending in direction of turn. Counter steering this way may not be instinctive but if not applied can result in the rider going where he most fears.

On a poor surface the back end may lose traction causing it to step out. In this attitude the traction forces are acting to help negotiate the bend somewhat like a speedway rider (who also uses the inside foot on the track to complete the stability picture).

The worst thing a rider can do is to shut the throttle

Untrained: your instinct will be to shut the throttle

If you do and the back wheel grips again, the bike will snap back into line violently "sitting up" and pitching the rider off in what is called a "high sider" after the direction in which the rider is thrown from the bike. It will hurt.

Better to keep on the gas even if you lean so far that you slide down onto the road…Do try to push the bike away from you before it lands on you if you do this…

At a sensible speed on a good dry road surface, the opposite will happen if you shut the throttle in a corner. The bike slows and therefore needs less lean for the same radius bend. It sits up but in a gentle manner.

If you use any front brake, assuming the surface is good, the effect will be the same but exaggerated and more rapid. If the surface is slippery you may find yourself at the mercy of your ABS. Without ABS and a finely tuned skill with front brake application, you will almost certainly drop the bike.

Slippery Surfaces

The key is to do nothing or as near to nothing as you can to make the bike deviate from a straight path. In the absence of braking and with a neutral throttle (neither on nor off the gas but exactly matching the road speed) the bike will not suddenly fall over. Gyroscopic effect will see to that. If you cannot rely on your throttle control, use the clutch but try to keep the engine revs matched.

Higher gears produce less torque at the rear wheel and less torque reaction which the tyres must ultimately provide. The exception is sand. The front wheel will not steer very well and you may need more aggressive use of the throttle to deliberately make the back end move out to point the whole bike in the right direction. This needs lots of torque and a lower gear. Not least because the rolling resistance is so high it can easily cause the bike to bog down, unless you force it out of the way rather like a circular saw!

- *Disclaimer*
- *Eyesight test*
- *POWERed checks*
- *Additional pre-ride checks*
- *Rider comfort and bike Fit*
- *Rider assessment*
- *Technique BEFORE speed*
- *Identify – analyse - remedy*

STUDENTS

DISCLAIMER IF APPLICABLE

Generally, there are two types of Trainer that deliver advanced rider training. Those that are paid for their services and those that are not. Having been on both sides of the fence, as a former police officer, I can state that an insurance certificate for professional indemnity is beneficial if charging for your services. In a voluntary capacity, representing an organisation, it is not uncommon and good practice, for a student to be given a formal disclaimer notice. This must be read, signed and dated by the student and countersigned by the Trainer. The disclaimer should be relevant to all training sessions undertaken and if appropriate, relevant for use by an Examiner on test. Check with your organisation that such a disclaimer is available.

EYESIGHT TEST

It is important for you to conduct an eyesight test of the

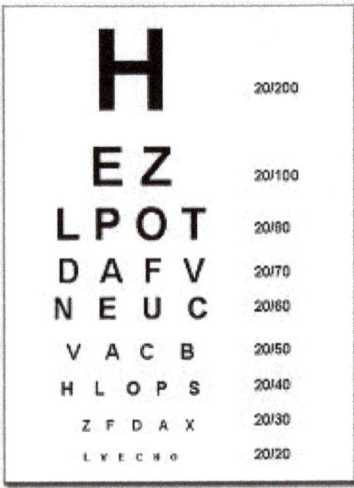

student before you ride with them. If spectacles or contact lenses are normally worn when riding, then they must be worn for the eyesight test. Locate a vehicle that is in line with the student that is 20 metres away (approximately four car lengths) and have them read out the registration number to you. If the student has difficulty in reading the number plate or cannot distinguish it to your satisfaction, then you must advise the student to seek professional advice about their eyesight. Do not undertake any on road training if you believe their eyesight is defective. On another cautionary note, be aware that this test is the minimum needed to meet driving licence requirements. It may well be that you discover on your rides that one or more of your students eyesight is lacking, particular for far distances. If this is the case, it makes sense to suspend training activities until the student has had their eyesight professionally examined.

POWERED CHECKS

These are basic visual checks of the student's motorbike to make sure it is legal and suitable to ride on the public road.

Complete the "POWERED" checks with the student. It is their bike; he or she should be familiar with it. Engage them in conversation, find out what they like about their bike and what they don't like about their bike. This is ideal as an "ice breaker" to make your conversation a two way process. Ask how often it is serviced and who does it. It is also very good to hear what is being said, as you will not have ridden every model of bike out there and you will also learn a lot about how they perform.

Explain the importance of the checks being made, especially if they have to use another bike, for example, one that is loaned whilst theirs is in for service. How will they know if it is roadworthy if they don't check it? The checks you want the student to conduct are:

Petrol   Ask the student what grade of fuel is used and how many litres does the tank hold. Is there a reserve tank? Most bikers know approximately how many miles they can ride before they must refuel. Does your student know how many, as you need to know if they have enough  fuel for your ride with them. It is quite common that the first time students meet with you, they say they need to fill up before you ride. You can prevent this by asking them to turn up for their appointment with sufficient fuel for the ride you have planned. If you don't the down time of refuelling will eat into your training period.

Oil   The student should know how to check the engine oil and brake fluid levels. Some bikes also have a reservoir for clutch fluid. Get them to explain and show you how it is checked. Does the student know where to put the oil in and if needed, how much? The bike may have a clear inspection glass for engine oil level or a screw out dipstick.   Refer to the  manufacturer's manual if you have difficulty in locating either. Brake fluid reservoirs may be found on the handlebars for the front brake and located on the frame towards the rear or under the seat, for the rear brake. Refer to the manufacturer's manual if you have difficulty in locating these.

Water   Some bikes are now water cooled. Does the student know how to check the radiator for leaks and check the fluid level regularly? Refer to the manufacturer's manual if you have difficulty in locating the filler cap.

Electrics   Ask your student to show you that all lights, horn, indicators and ancillary equipment are in working order. Check that they carry spare bulbs and fuses. If a bulb fails can they demonstrate how to give arm signals for slowing down, turning right and left?

Rubber   Tyres are what keep the bike on the road. It is vitally important that they are checked regularly. Generally, if there is something wrong with the tyre, there is a law for it and you could end up with points on the rider's licence for the defect.   Have your student check that there is sufficient tread on the tyres across their width and circumference. Do they conform to the legal limit? Ask the student what is the correct tyre pressure, as recommended by the bike manufacturer.   Ask how often they check the pressures and if they know that they should do this when the tyres are cold. If

tyre pressures are incorrect, the bike will never handle properly. Standard pressures are given for a wide range of rider weight and road conditions.   If your student carries a passenger or luggage, the pressures may need to be increased.   Look for uneven wear, sidewalls split, bulges, exposed cords, damage to wheel rims and check that tyre valve caps are fitted.

Equipment   Check the student is suitably dressed in helmet, textile or leather clothing, gloves and boots. The legal requirement may only require the wearing of a crash helmet but any rider who realises the risks associated with riding will always wear full protective equipment, appropriate for the weather conditions. Most riders know what to do in wet and cold weather to protect themselves from the elements. In Cyprus the sun is a major hazard. Without protection for the eyes, the glare can be intense and make riders squint, which greatly reduces their vision. If gloves are not worn, severe sunburn can be expected to hands and wrists.

Damage   Particularly with replacement bikes or bikes that are shared with others, you must check for any damage to the bike which cannot be accounted for, or which could be considered dangerous, for example twisted handlebars.   Get your student to do a comprehensive visual check of their bike in your presence.

Your student does not want anything falling off while riding.   Neither do you, as you will be right behind him or her.

Things to look out for are; is the seat secure, fork travel correct with no leaks, handlebars secure, no free play in the swinging arm, the chain is not too tight or too loose and the sprockets are not worn with rounded teeth, no play in the driveshaft, no cracks in the frame welds, sufficient "meat" on the brake pads, no leaks in brake hoses, brake and clutch levers, no detioriation of rubber bushes, loose spokes, fractures to wheels, exhaust mountings are secure, mirrors etc? And talking about mirrors - have your student check them to make sure they are securely fixed, correctly positioned and clean to give a clear view behind.   If they have cracks, the view will be distorted and be a distraction to your student.

ADDITIONAL PRE-RIDE CHECKS

Ride at approximately 25mph (40kph) and brake progressively and firmly to make sure the brakes are effective and the bike stops in a straight line.

The POWERED check, although very good to implement before a ride, really only gives a rider an overview of the condition of their bike. As a Trainer, you should have an understanding of how bikes work in more detail.   It is not unreasonable to expect this from your students either, as some of the additional checks undertaken can improve performance and stability of their bike. This will increase their confidence and help them to understand that there is much more to riding than point and squirt!

Lots of bikes can be fine-tuned to make the handling of the bike safer and smoother so that the rider performs well. If a rider pays particular attention to their bike, they will also recognise when components on their bike are starting to fail or going beyond their normal life. It is far better to maintain and replace components than let them go beyond their designed or intended lifetime. They will not last forever and no rider should ever experience a mechanical failure or items dropping off at speed through neglect or false economy. It can hurt and cost a lot more in the end.

SUSPENSION

Just like tyres, the front forks and the rear shock absorber(s) are responding to the road surface to provide stability and grip. They are constantly hard at work and will, at some stage, start to degrade, so the ride may become stiffer or a lot floatier. One thing is for sure, the bike will not feel right. If that is the case, the shock absorbers will need some attention or replacement.

If the bike has been owned since new for more than three years or, when purchased, was over three years old, then it could be time for the shock absorbers to be serviced or replaced. Rear shock linkages should also be cleaned, checked and lubricated. Upgrades to the suspension of a bike are often considered to improve the suspension and let a rider have a greater range of adjustment. It can completely transform a bike.

If the suspension can be adjusted, it is always best to read the manufacturers settings to find out what suits the needs of the rider. A good tip is to write down the settings before adjustments are made, so you can always go back to where you started. This may be the best option. The rear set-up is more critical to get right compared to the front, so it is best to get that right first.

After initial adjustment, only change one thing at a time (preload, compression or rebound) and ride the bike to find out what makes an improvement.

CHAIN

The harder a bike is ridden, the more the chain is put under stress. The quicker the chain will then stretch and increase wear on the sprockets eventually resulting in rounded teeth and a risk of the chain coming off. No rider would want to experience a chain wrapping itself around the rear wheel.

Check the handbook to see how the chain is adjusted to take up any slack. The chain should not be too tight or too loose because it affects the rear suspension and this in turn can result in handling problems. Regular checks, combined with sympathetic throttle use will ensure longer chain and sprockets life.

Make sure it is lubricated and cleaned to maximise its life.

BRAKES

Brake pads are very easy to check visually by looking into the callipers to check the thickness of the pads. If a rider has some basic mechanical knowledge, it is a simple task to replace or clean them. Always remember that if they are removed pump the brake lever or foot pedal after replacing them so that the pistons take up their normal operating position. If this is not done, when the time comes to use them for the first time, there will be a heart stopping rather than bike stopping moment. Perhaps, even a need for some clean underwear. The pads will initially fail to bite the discs and slow the bike down. A second or even a third squeeze of the lever by a, now panicking, rider may then result in too much pressure being applied, followed by loss of control of the bike.

An advanced rider always gets up to speed in a progressive manner. Engine, tyres, brakes and fluids all warm up gradually. Heavy braking on a cold disc could warp them as they rapidly heat up.

Brake fluid degrades over time. It loses its ability to function and may result in brake fade. The pressure on the brake lever or pedal will then feel soft and spongy. The bike will take more time and distance to slow down. In worst case scenarios the lever or pedal may need to be pumped to get some pressure into the system to get the brakes to work. Old fluid will also cause the seals in the system to degrade which will result in costly repairs.

RIDER COMFORT, LEVERS AND ADJUSTMENTS

Size and build of a rider should be considered when choosing a bike as one size does not suit all. You may have to live with your purchase for quite a while so it is worthwhile being realistic with your options and  have a good idea what you want to get out of biking for your budget.

For one of the authors, the appeal of a sports bike falls far short of what can reasonably be accepted to ride safely and comfortably. At two metres tall and weighing 110 kilos, sitting astride a sports bike, moulding to its shape brings on all sorts of pains, aches and cramps. We must also ride it out of the showroom! Better to choose a large engined and faired tourer.

Dependant on the type of bike ridden, there may be adjustments that can make the riding position more comfortable. Whilst most bikes can usually provide adjustments for brake, clutch, gear levers and seat, some also allow adjustment of foot pegs and handlebars. Most bikes' brake and clutch levers are capable of being adjusted to suit the reach of a rider's fingers. Correctly adjusted, this can minimise wrist ache, even when riding a sport's bike.

The same goes for the gear lever. If it can be adjusted, do so. There is nothing worse than a gear lever that is too high or too low, resulting in awkward gear changes and an ache in the ankle.

Check for free play in the throttles and adjust this at the twist grip if it possible to do so.

A bit of research will also reveal aftermarket devices which can be fitted to a bike to make it more comfortable. One of the authors did this to lower his foot pegs. This reduced his back ache and leg cramps and made gear changing easier. The money spent was well worthwhile and he now has the perfect bike.

Finally, clean the bike. You cannot see the defects in a dirty bike. This puts you at risk from potential tyre damage, unseen leaks and cracked or damaged frame and suspension.

ASSESSING RIDER SKILL

Having completed the eyesight and POWERED checks it's time to settle the student down in readiness for their assessment ride. Their riding style will be unique to them and that includes good or bad habits or a combination of both. In fact, some of their thought processes may already be that of an advanced rider, they have just never recognised it or have never been told.

Reassure the student that this is not a test. Far from it, you need them to ride their bike as they would do normally. They shouldn't revert to how they were taught to ride or ride to impress. Put them at their ease and encourage them to be themselves. But guess what? The student will find it difficult to relax, be nervous because they are under scrutiny and be unnecessarily hesitant, unless that is already part of their makeup.

RULES OF THE RIDE

Your student will need frequent input from you about what to do. This applies whether you are just observing your student or are in training mode. If your student does not understand what you want from them, the session will become very disjointed. You, therefore, must have a mutual understanding between you and your student(s) for every ride. Think of the safety procedure before you fly, it is the same principle. You are giving out information for the safety of your ride.

Just like giving directions, if you work to a script you are less likely to miss anything and it will become second nature for you to communicate the rules of the ride. First, always specify the student who you want to lead the ride. An example of what to say would be;

"David, you will ride in front, number one position. I will ride behind you in number two position (if you have more students and we would suggest there are no more than two others, they would ride in position three and four). I will direct you where to go. Ride as if you were on your own, do what you would do normally (as your training progresses with your student you can change the second part of your sentence to *as you have been trained*). Do not be influenced by the presence or positioning of myself or any other rider behind you. If you turn out of a road and I am unable to follow, carry on with your ride. I am in radio contact with you, I know our route and if I am unable to keep you in sight, I will radio to you to pull up on the left in a safe and convenient place. Do you understand?"

If the student confirms they understand, then ask them politely to repeat your instructions. If they have any doubts then repeat the rules of the ride.

Now that you are ready to go all that needs to be said is, "David, ride on when you're ready please".

THE ASSESSMENT OR FIRST RIDE

- *Observation rather than training*
- *Look at machine control, hazard awareness, speed and positioning*
- *Prioritise one or two aspects to address*
- *Your process:-*
    - *Identify the issue(s)*
    - *Analyse the cause(s)*
    - *Determine the potential remedies*

Generally, when you ride with a student for the first time it is an observed ride where no training is taking place but in order to get from A to B you are giving directions, preferably over a radio. At the conclusion of this ride and having fed back to your student, your presence and time with him or her now becomes that of Trainer. You will be communicating with your student on the move to improve their riding skills in every aspect of their ride.

The time you spend with a student will vary greatly. Some riders may only wish to spend a few hours or a full day or two with you. Others may meet up with you over a period of time which, usually, is the way to progress to an advanced riding test. From the outset you will have to decide which aspects of their riding behaviour you wish to prioritise. For example, you are concentrating on how to ride bends. You have had a question and answer session followed up by a briefing on the subject. A lot of information has to be retained and put into practice by your student. He or she will be focused on the task to do well.

So what happens during the ride when the student is confronted by a situation you have not discussed or briefed on? What are you going to do? Imagine the following situation. Your student exits a bend and has sufficient speed to overtake one or more vehicles in front of him or her. This is where you can radio to the student, "If you wish to overtake, do what you would do normally". This is not a way to avoid dealing with the situation. It is the safest thing to do; do not be tempted to talk the student through how to do an overtaking manoeuvre. You will have plenty of opportunities to do so later on. Sit back and watch how the student executes the manoeuvre or not. It is good information for you to recall at your next break and for when you are both ready to deal with this subject in more depth.

DURING THE RIDE

Within a few minutes you will recognise whether or not they have undergone any advanced rider training. Think IPSGA and it all falls into place. The student will probably be reactive, not proactive. He or she will, probably, position their bike incorrectly. Their forward and rearward observations may be inadequate but most importantly, go with your gut feeling as to how well or poorly they perform with their awareness and anticipation skills...you will not be wrong!

So how long should the assessment ride take? It should take into account the variety in the road network available to you. This will take time. You should have a route ready to assess their skill level, which will take approximately 40 minutes.

Traffic density i.e. in a city or town, will be good for a multitude of hazards in a slow moving environment. But the road situation changes rapidly, so whilst speed may be slow, decision making has to be very fast. The suburbs, which lead out onto the open road, are totally different. The student can ride faster, as traffic volume decreases, but in comparison to the town environment, are they a better or worse rider. More importantly, are they consistent in their riding behaviour, irrespective of the road they find themselves on.

The secret to advanced rider training, for assessments and further development, is being able to:

- **Identify** the fault – **what** is it that is incorrect or could be done better?
- **Analyse** the fault – **why** is it happening, why are they doing it?
- Provide the route to **remedy** – provide a solution to the student describing **how** to overcome the fault

For example:

- **Identify** – braking is late and harsh
- **Analyse** – reacting to the presence of other road users too late
- **Remedy** – better forward vision, increased awareness and anticipation will allow more time for the student to brake smoothly and progressively

AT THE END OF THE ASSESSMENT

Ideally, you will have chosen a quiet spot in which to park up and discuss what you have observed. Now is the time to provide some verbal feedback to the student.

Usually, the student has an acceptable level of riding skill and expertise. You need to assess their true ability, in order to develop their potential, by rectifying their bad habits and imparting new skills. By asking them **why** they do something and listening to their answer, you will understand why they exhibit such riding behaviour.

So what was good, what was not so good, what was bad or dangerous?

The feedback should only last a few minutes. Be positive in what you are going to say. Keep your choice of words simple and effective, the less said the better. Whatever you say will be retained better by the person you're talking to. Do not expect them always to remember all the things you noticed, as they were really concentrating on their ride and may experience difficulty in recollecting what you saw.

If the student displayed a riding habit that you consider to be dangerous, then this should be the first topic you discuss with them; for example, excessive use of speed. Verify the knowledge and skill of the student and brief on the habit(s) that you wish to rectify. Remember to outline the aims and objectives that will achieve this and ask them to verbally feedback to you what is expected from the training period.

USE OF SPEED

Throughout your training you will need to impress upon your students that "*technique comes before speed*".

As the student advances, the speed can be increased safely. This can only be done with careful consideration for the prevailing circumstances, including legislation and its local enforcement.

RIDER DEVELOPMENT

- *Talk through IPSGA*
- *Use Q&A to determine understanding*
- *Correlate IPSGA to issues identified in the assessment*
- *Remember BRIEF – PROMPT - PRAISE*
- *Don't let errors become habits*

Now you are ready for your next ride, probably to return to the location where you met your student. The scanning technique is an ideal topic to start with. Generally, it takes a considerable amount of time to perfect this technique. It is also the logical way to introduce the system of IPSGA with "Information" being the first phase of the system. Provide a brief explanation of what scanning is and how it is achieved and let the ride begin.

CONTINUED DEVELOPMENT

RECTIFYING RIDING ERRORS

As your student progresses, with radio communications, you will be able to correct errors on the move. For example, the student forgets to do lifesavers. Bring it to their attention and tell them to rectify the error. Put them into situations where they have to do lifesavers to ensure they demonstrate the technique correctly.

Should something happen during the ride that you feel cannot be discussed on the move, then tell the student to remember what just occurred, so that it can be discussed later when you stop for a break.

At any time, revisit any aspect of training if any ambiguity or inconsistency arises.

The skill of a good Trainer is the ability to identify the true cause of errors that students make.   For example, a student approaches a junction and brakes late.   A Trainer has to identify, analyse and provide sufficient guidance to rectify the error and ensure it doesn't persist.   If the error is not properly identified, it will be repeated.

The Trainer will have to decide whether any error occurred through lack of awareness, anticipation, poor observation or the student's practical bike riding skills by observing his or her riding action and behaviour.   It is also possible that more than one aspect needs remedy, for example poor observations and poor braking technique.

Your own training as a Trainer will provide you with the skill to correctly identify riding errors, so you can give your students the correct information to rectify them.

You must always be prepared for questions from students on any riding matters.   You'll be surprised at what they may ask in order to increase their knowledge.

EVALUATION STOPS

To pay attention for any length of time, with full concentration, we humans need to be rested, fed and watered. Even then, we can only concentrate for a short time.

Advanced rider training is intense for both student and Trainer. Stop regularly; then, if necessary, attend to these needs before proceeding with the de-briefing.

In any case stop between 45 minutes and 1 hour duration to take a break. It will be very much appreciated.

Remember, both you and your students also need to be relaxed, that is to say not preoccupied with something else, interested in the material, motivated and not distracted by other calls on your attention.

As a Trainer, you need to bear the above in mind for your briefing and de-briefing stops and any intermediate stops. Typically, it is better to consider having food and drink first!

ADDRESS ANY FAULTS WHENEVER YOU STOP

Whenever you stop for a break, use it as an opportunity to give feedback on the ride so far. This is particularly the case when you need to say more than can be reasonably communicated on the move. What you say may result in a question and answer session to clarify a characteristic of the ride and it may need significant input from you. This is where a notebook and pen becomes extremely useful, enabling you to be more descriptive. Now you can outline your observations and what can be done to make the ride better. Do not be surprised if the student asks to use your pad and pen too, as they also benefit from using it to better explain their thinking or actions. This is a simple idea but it works well because you bring your words to life, which gets your message across more effectively and quicker too.

For example, your student is stopping and looking both ways before he or she emerges from a minor road into a major road with give way signs. The student is focused on the mouth of the junction. He or she is riding as if to stop at the give way line even though all-round visibility is good. They intend to stop because they have not properly observed what is coming from each direction. Your student has missed the opportunities, on the approach to the junction, to make sufficient observations by not using an effective scanning technique to assess the junction, to emerge safely without stopping.

Explain where you would be looking for Information, using every opportunity to enable you to assess the junction better and earlier, on approach, to control your speed, to make your final assessment as to whether or not it is safe to go.

This way you are passing on your own skills and knowledge to assist them, so the next time they do this, you will quickly recognise that they put into practice what you said and display their new found knowledge. As they practice more and more, it will become consistent and their old habit will disappear.

For example, you want to clarify and discuss the use of indicators and the timing of them. At the end of the briefing, ask the student to feed back to you what they are going to do, so that any ambiguity can be cleared up before the student rides off.

During the ride, if you feel something needs to be discussed immediately consider stopping the student and pull up in a safe and convenient place to discuss it.

REMEMBER...

- IDENTIFY the fault - what did you see?
- ANALYSE it - why did it happen?
- RECTIFY it - give advice and guidance as to how to make it better
- PRAISE – if no faults are displayed or consistency of managing the task is of a high standard, it is good practice to give positive feedback and praise to let the student know how well they performed. By reinforcing what you have seen, it will increase the confidence of the student and they will recognise the importance of keeping their standards up.

More importantly, when a student is at this skill level or approaching it, you will have empowered them to analyse their own riding ability. It is extremely rewarding as a Trainer to hear from your student that they have enjoyed their ride but recognise what they can do to make it better and take pleasure in discussing it with you.

STAGE 1 -TALK THROUGH AND GUIDANCE

After a question and answer session and briefing on any topic, the knowledge and advice you offered has to be put into practice. Your role now is to observe and/or talk your student(s) through the exercise. As an example, the topic being taught is how to approach, negotiate and exit roundabouts. The route should encompass as many variations of roundabouts as possible, including mini roundabouts.

Your role is to give verbal instruction on observations, use of speed, priority in roundabouts, positioning and signalling and more whilst the student negotiates the roundabout.

Having completed this exercise several times, stop and debrief the student on their performance.

STAGE 2 - PROMPTING

The student is encouraged to deal with roundabouts based on their knowledge and the practical experience you have provided. Your role is to support and give verbal instruction as and when the student experiences some difficulty or forgets the techniques taught.

Having completed this exercise several times, stop and debrief the student on their performance. Then you can ride to let your student perfect their skill.

STAGE 3 - DISPLAY OF KNOWLEDGE AND SKILL OF TOPIC BY STUDENT

The student is encouraged to deal with roundabouts and display that they can use their knowledge and riding skills, whilst you observe their ability to do so.

Having completed this exercise several times, stop and debrief the student on their performance.

WHAT WORKS?

We are actively involved in training riders in advanced riding skills and have trained riders in readiness to take their advanced riding tests, although not everyone may wish to do so. Our training is structured to ensure riders are prepared and confident to take a test or to reach a standard they are comfortable with to gain maximum enjoyment from their riding adventures.

Our expertise has proven that a maximum time period of twenty hours training adequately prepares most students for their advanced riding test. To develop consistently proficient skills, the student must also practice what they have learnt between sessions. Dependent upon individual ability and the feedback we provide in a student's progress, an informed decision can be made if a student is ready for test. Generally, it works well to meet up with a student for ten sessions of two hours minimum duration. The assessment ride is not part of the twenty hours development.

There is no time scale to adhere to from start of development to test date. For example, some people may only take ten weeks whilst others may take a year. You will also need to consider your personal schedule, availability and commitment of the student to progress to a successful conclusion. Flexibility has been the key to our success.

REALITY CHECK

With this in mind, it must also be recognised that, at some stage during a student's development, even with the strongest support from a Trainer, the possibility of a student not being suitable for test still exists. You are doing your best.   Your student, for whatever reason, just is not, or cannot apply themselves to the task in hand.

Therefore, it would be unreasonable and unfair for them to take an advanced riding test and pay the test fee. Especially, if in your opinion, they would probably fail their test.   Your professionalism to provide feedback, even if it may be hard to accept, must be honest and truthful. You will be respected for your openness and your student will have undoubtedly gained from your input in helping them to improve their standard of riding.

If you are operating under an IAM or RoSPA scheme, there may be an opportunity to seek a second opinion from an Examiner, to review your assessment and, if appropriate, for an Examiner to discuss or assess the student's ability and readiness for test. If operating as a group or business, this might be done by using a colleague or peer.

TIPS TO MONITOR AND SUPPORT PROGRESS

Every training session must:

- start with a review of the previous training session
- include a briefing for the current session
- provide feedback during the session
- provide feedback at the conclusion of the session
- result in a verbal agreement from the student that they will practice the riding skills necessary to move on in readiness for their next session

Generally, after six hours training, a distinct improvement in a student's progress will be recognised.

After twelve hours, a student's progress and potential to take a test at a future date becomes apparent. At the sixth training session it is very productive to spend a few moments to explain where a student is in their development. You can refresh their memory about what the advanced riding test entails. Do not hold back in what you wish to tell your student...tell him or her their true potential. Be truthful and honest. People will spend a lot of money to take their test and the reality is that not everyone will pass.

The time between fourteen to eighteen hours allows a student to build on their strengths, to maintain consistency. They are preparing for a test and should want to deliver their best performance. Again, be truthful after every session and advise them as to their potential to pass a test. More importantly, clearly identify what they have to do or perfect to achieve their goal.

Having completed sixteen hours training with a student, if appropriate, have another Trainer or Examiner check the performance of your student. This is for comparison and your peace of mind, to confirm that you and your student are on the right track. The check is not a training session.

After eighteen hours, you must advise your student to review their own performance. Is there anything they are unsure or concerned about? Would they like some more development in a particular aspect from you? Let them think about it before booking the final session. Put the onus on them. This reinforces the fact that you are considering every eventuality and providing them with a failsafe opportunity to be fully prepared for test. For you, there is nothing more rewarding, knowing you have done the best for them and to hear that they are ready to go.

The final two hours, of your twenty hours of training, should concentrate on at least two short rides with no feedback on the move.   At the conclusion of each ride, provide feedback to the student.   Now is the time for the student to decide if they wish to apply for their test.

WHAT IF A STUDENT'S PROGRESS IS NOT UP TO EXPECTATIONS?

Remember the clock is ticking.   As more training sessions are completed, there will be less time for a student to fully prepare for their test.   Part of your responsibilities in readiness for this will be to ensure:

- you have provided the student with information on how to book a test

- you are confident that your student understands what will be expected of them on test

- your student is fully competent to recognise a fault in their performance, rectify it and remain in control during their test

- your student understands that Examiners do not ask trick questions.   What they do is to ask questions to verify the thought processes, actions and behaviour of test candidates in how they dealt with a particular hazard.   The expectation is that their reply will offer a reasoned account to confirm they were pro-active, not re-active, to any situation or hazard they were confronted with

- your student is capable of providing an informed response, based on knowledge of Motorcycle Roadcraft, the System and the implementation of it

SAFEGUARDS FOR TRAINERS IN READINESS FOR A STUDENT'S ADVANCED TEST

A student's development should not overlook the obvious. This is easily dealt with by a question and answer session and, if necessary, supported with practical input.

For example, it is very easy to accept that your student, who has been riding for many years, can deal with roundabouts. But can they? Imagine he or she takes their test and their skill level is lacking and it affects their performance on test. The Examiner feeds back to them and he or she replies, "We didn't cover that". How will they feel? What will they think of your performance as a Trainer? What about the Organisation's reputation? How will you explain yourself?

There are two things you can do to safeguard yourself against this happening. First, maintain notes of a student's performance for you to refer to as they progress. It is also helpful to refer to them for a pre-ride briefing, to check the student is up to speed and has not forgotten anything. If you wish, you can also give your student a copy of them to refer to whilst they practice in between training sessions.

Secondly, keep a checklist of the topics you have trained them in. The checklist (Appendix 1) is what we use and a box is only ticked when a student has acquired and can display the skill and knowledge required of that particular topic. An un-ticked box means there is some more work to do. A checklist that has been fully ticked means that you and your student can agree that all has been done in readiness for them to take their test. You will make notes and keep a checklist won't you?

TRAINING SESSIONS FOR BENDS

INTRODUCTION OF A NEW TOPIC

As an example, we will consider how bends are safely ridden and the importance of recognition of the limit point and the exit point. The student may not know anything at all about this subject and if that is the case, it has to be taught from scratch. A question and answer session to find out what your student knows about this topic should be the first thing to take place. Now let us assume a briefing is needed on the topic before the ride is started.

- *Start with a briefing*
- *Use Q&A and draw diagrams as needed*
- *Bends – walk one to make limit points and hazards real in slow time*
- *Show how IPSGA is applied*
- *Explain typical errors and why they occur*

Diagrams and/or photos of bends will assist with your briefing. Consider walking a bend to put what you say into a visual context. We always find this very beneficial.

When the briefing is over and the student is riding, you can now help them by:

- allowing them to display they can put the knowledge into practice and undertake the task on their own initiative

- revisit the previous training if any ambiguity or inconsistency arises
- if needed, demonstrate the task on your own bike and have them follow you
- you will have afforded the student the opportunity to put the knowledge into practice and gradually the practice delivers consistency

So now you will have introduced a new subject and have passed on your knowledge. Staying with the topic of bends, we have expanded on the subject of bend tuition because it is the hazard which results in the highest casualty rate for bikers when it goes wrong. It is also a complicated subject which cannot be taught in a single session and illustrates the general approach and logic to training a complex topic or subject.

The list of topics for bend tuition below needs to be broken down into manageable session content. Here is a question for you. "How do you eat an elephant?" Answer, "One bite at a time." During each session use the events and the behaviours exhibited by your student to expand on the chosen topics. For example, if the student appears to have difficulty holding the correct line through the bend or series of bends, it might lead to a discussion on gear selection, use of gas, counter steering or scanning technique.

POINTS TO COVER IN A BRIEFING ON BENDS
- How the student should put IPSGA into practice for bends?
- Limit point – how is it identified?
- Exit point – how is it identified?
- Sacrifice position for safety – what does this mean?

- Correct use of speed – what happens to speed in a bend?
- Gear – correct use of gear for acceleration, road holding, on the level, uphill and downhill
- Use of gas – how is throttle used and when can power be applied?
- Counter steering – what is it, how is it used?
- Use of mirrors – when?
- Braking in a bend – which one can the student use, how much pressure?
- Double apex – what will happen?
- Straight lining – is it acceptable? – if so, to what degree and what observations must be undertaken before committing to the manoeuvre ?
- Acceleration sense between bends
- Braking technique approaching bends

ERRORS THAT STUDENTS DISPLAY...

- Late positioning on approach
- Too fast on entry
- Too slow on entry
- Not sacrificing position for safety
- Braking in a bend
- Right and left bends – turning in too early
- Not identifying the exit for early position out of the bend
- Too high a gear
- Too slow riding the bend
- Not enough lean
- Not counter steering
- Going off line in bend
- Vision dropping
- Not using mirrors before entering or having exited the bend

RIGHT HAND BENDS ARE HARDER TO RIDE

There are plenty of riders that have miscalculated their speed and positioning, reacted badly and found themselves going off the road in a right hand bend. That is an expensive and painful mistake to make and yet many riders will repeat this experience, never giving it a thought that they actually need some professional guidance to avoid it happening again. Sadly, too many riders make this mistake only once. Your student may need more time to master how they ride a right hand bend. Their position on approach may be good but the turn into the bend may be too early. Why is that? The answer is simple, they are riding too fast. They reach the bend and then react to it. They are turning in too early

to ride away from the apparent danger which is the bend ahead of them. They do not want to find themselves going straight ahead and off the road. Self preservation kicks in, they slow down and steer away.

When a rider turns in too early into a right hand bend, they move towards the centre of the road and could cross onto the opposite side. This is not a good place to be when an oncoming vehicle approaches. The rider will have to steer left and might even have to brake, to lose speed to get back to their side of the road. The bike will become unstable and it is an unpleasant experience for a rider. Hasn't every rider made that mistake? So what is it that they are doing wrong?

The answer is simple; they are riding too fast, have not recognised the limit point and are staring ahead. The bike they are riding is running out of road. If they remain focused in front of them, the chances are they will go straight ahead. The bend is reached and then the student reacts to it. They are turning in too early to ride away from the apparent danger, which is the bend ahead of them. They do not want to find themselves going straight ahead and off the road.

The way to correct this habit is for you to get your student to practice riding in to the entry slowly, maintaining their position to the left and, when the exit is reached, to accelerate out of the bend. This is where the use of the limit point works exceptionally well to assess the correct use of speed to negotiate a bend. Can they identify the limit point and do they know how to use it to their advantage? Many Trainers will try to explain how this works verbally. Do not be surprised that, if you do adopt this practice, your student will take a considerable amount of time to acquire this skill. It will also take up a lot of your time explaining, over and over again, the technique before the penny drops.

MotoGP riders walk the circuit! Why shouldn't you and your student do likewise? Go to a quiet road, park up and walk round the bend to see the view of the road ahead and what a limit point actually looks like. Your student will be able to see how the nearside verge/kerb meets the offside verge/kerb to look like an arrow head shape. By walking the bend towards the limit point, your student will be able to see if it remains stationary or moves. If it does not move, you can tell the student that they must slow down until it moves away. Whilst walking the bend you, will also be able to brief on how IPSGA works and how the student can maintain speed and stability throughout the bend when the limit point moves, until they see the exit point.

You can explain that the exit point is where the nearside verge/kerb and offside verge/kerb separate again and the road surface reappears between them. Now the student knows when to straighten up to exit the bend, can re-position the bike on the road and use more gas to ride out of the bend under controlled acceleration.

With the briefing over, you can observe your student on a ride to see how they deal with bends. Get the student to ride at a speed which allows them time, space and attention to plan their approach. They must identify the limit point and when to start the turn into the bend. To ride into the bend and then react is too late.

As this is a right hand bend exercise, they should aim to approach the corner on the left hand side of their lane. This should not be so close to the edge as to distract them by worrying about staying on the road but about one metre from the edge of the tarmac is good to begin with. Remember, they may need to sacrifice position for safety too.

Your student should be scanning, to recognise the limit point and control their speed on approach to the bend. Get them to use acceleration sense or apply the brake(s) and stay off the gas until the limit point is seen to move away. Now is the time to select a gear for the road speed and put on some gas to ride the bike around the bend at an even speed. They should enter the bend with a margin for error, keeping their speed down. The student can accelerate if the bend turns out to be easier but, if it is a tightening bend, a slower speed is safer. Once the exit point is seen and the bike is stable, more power can be used to ride away.

When radioing commands or providing feedback on the move whilst riding bends be selective as to when you communicate. Make sure there is sufficient distance and time for you to say what you want and for your student to respond to it. When you exit a bend, you will know by scanning the road ahead and from personal experience, if it is achievable to communicate before entering the next bend. If not just remain quiet, don't be tempted to speak, otherwise you will have to cut off mid sentence and it becomes rather messy.

ADVANCED VERSUS RACING LINES THROUGH BENDS

The fastest way round a bend is a racing line. Unfortunately, on the public highway this is also the fastest way to kill yourself, any pillion and any other road users you collide with.

Why and what is the difference?

Let us consider a left hand bend on a two way road on which you drive on the left.

For the racing line you want to create an apex where you will be travelling slowest at a point just after you have finished braking. You will be just on the gas and as you see the bend open up towards the exit you will accelerate as hard as the bend allows. You will approach the apex as far to the right as possible, apex close to the left hand edge but it is unlikely to be at the edge unless the shape of the bend is such that it is convenient to create the apex there.

On the race track you can use all the road and traffic is one way. Even if the bend is "blind" there is a relatively small chance of other hazards than the bend itself and the behaviour of other racers who may force you to pick a different apex to the optimum for maximum speed.

Back to the public highway: you can only go as far to the right as the law (solid white lines) or oncoming traffic allows. The exit will also be similarly restricted so your apex will necessarily be less than optimum. Worse...if you choose an apex near the left edge of the road your vision may be limited by obstacles such as building, vegetation or street furniture (road signs, bollards, crash barriers etc.) If you are travelling as fast as the apex will permit (not visibility or other factors) you will have no choice but to go to the right as you get on the gas and accelerate out of the bend. To keep further to the left you must be travelling slower. But if your vision was restricted you do not know what is there...like an oncoming car on the wrong side of the road. Now where are you going to go? Your choices may be severely restricted. Going nowhere fast?

If you had taken the advanced line you would have stayed as far right as possible until you could see the exit completely with all its hazards; fixed, moving and weather. Your speed would be the safe maximum or slower throughout. You would have created flexibility and choice throughout the bend. The freedom to change position, adjust speed up or down. You would have removed stress and drama for you and anyone near you using that road.

The time difference is most likely measured in fractions of a second. Your life expectancy...that is measured in years!

SPECIAL TRAINING SESSIONS

- *Slow riding – looking where you want to go and using the rear brake*
- *Town riding – the hazards*
- *Filtering*
- *Overtaking safely*

Just because a student has a full driving licence it does not mean you can take it for granted that they have the requisite skill set to ride their bike. A good question and answer session and a thorough assessment will reveal all. It can be an eye opener to discover the lack of expertise a student will display. Do not be surprised at what you discover, talk things through with your student and then you can train them to a level of competence to perfect the shortfall(s) in their skill set.

There are three areas of riding skill which we have chosen to give more input to on how to develop the skills of a student. They surface time after time and it is not the fault of the student. The Instructor who trained them neglected to perfect their riding ability in one or more of these areas. The skills were never truly passed onto the student who was fortunate enough, if that is the correct word to use, to be picked up on during their test.

The areas we will deal with are:

- Slow riding
- Filtering
- Overtaking

SLOW RIDING AND USE OF REAR BRAKE

The distinguishing feature of a two wheeled vehicle is that it is less stable than four wheels. It is not stable unless it is on its stand or is moving. Easily proved by bringing a bike to a stop, keep your feet on the pegs and fall over. That is an expensive experiment to conduct. It takes a lot of skill to keep a bike upright at slow speed, travelling in a straight line. If it is ridden even slower, there is a risk of the bike stalling unless the clutch is pulled in. That is, unless the rider controls the clutch at biting point and the gas is sufficiently used to control the revs of the engine so the bike can creep along. Now introduce steering and it becomes more difficult.

Even after mastering this, there is something else the rider has to consider to be able to control their stability and speed. The use of the rear brake, gently applied, creates drag and helps to keep the bike stable. Too much and, obviously, the bike will come to a stop, so care has to be used when using it. So there we are, a student needs to co-ordinate the clutch, gas and rear brake to remain stable at slow speed.

We are not finished yet. There is something else the rider has to do to be proficient at slow riding. That is, to look where they want to go. The hands will follow the eyes and at slow speed that sometimes means turning the head, something riders do not want to do whilst they try to master this skill. There is enough going on already and you then ask them to look in an area they don't want to. They will get there in the end; to confidently turn their bike around, ride figures of eight and emerge from side roads without heading for the kerb directly opposite them.

When coming to a stop, increased pressure on the rear brake brings the bike gently to a controlled stop. By keeping pressure on the pedal, it is much like having the handbrake on in a car. The bike is secure on the road. The student can then put their left foot down on the road to prevent their bike toppling over.

A good exercise to perfect this technique is to find a quiet road or off road area, where the student can practice this. It helps to walk alongside a student, on their left, so you can keep an eye on how they use the clutch, you can hear the engine revs and allow about a metre distance between you both. Vary your walking pace up and down and get the student to keep up or slow down with you. Do not let your pace go so quickly that the clutch can be let fully out or you will be left standing, or have to break into a trot to keep up. You may need to talk them through what to do. Do this correctly and within a few moments, you will both appreciate how effective this exercise is.

At slow speeds, if the more powerful front brake is used, it will probably result in bringing the bike to an immediate stop. This sudden loss of speed can catch a student out, who then puts out both legs and puts their feet on the ground to keep upright, as it is about the only thing they can do in so short a space of time. The stop is not controlled and does not instil confidence in a rider.

Generally, when riding in a slower moving environment below 30kph, with good scanning techniques, increased awareness and anticipation levels, an advanced rider finds the use of the rear bike is sufficient for most braking needs. So, if a student is losing speed using front or front and rear brake, as the speed reduces, the pressure can be released on the front brake. Any further loss of speed can be controlled with the use of the rear brake.

When coming to a stop, a word of caution about the choice of foot to place on the ground once stopped. One of our student's told of the time when, on a group ride, they stopped at the side of the road for one of them to adjust something on a bike. The side stand was put out and the bike leaned to the left, except the bike kept falling as the road surface was not where it was thought to be. It had a steep camber. The student was caught off balance and fell off into the storm drain alongside the road, which was about one metre deep and assumed the position of an upturned tortoise. Then, to add insult to injury, the bike dropped in too. Fortunately, there were enough riders on hand to pull out the embarrassed rider and machine, after they had controlled their fits of laughter.

FILTERING

One of the great benefits of riding is being able to move through the traffic when it is congested and continue on your way. A bike takes up less space than other vehicles, is able to navigate narrow gaps and pass alongside vehicles or between lines of traffic. No unnecessary waste of time sitting in traffic for riders. That is if they can filter through traffic safely.

So what does that entail exactly? Well, it has to be given a lot of thought as to safety before committing to filter and local knowledge of road layouts helps immensely. Common sense, reasonableness, showing consideration to other road users and whether or not the action of filtering is legal, must be considered. Also, more importantly and this fact is often overlooked, a rider is reliant on the goodwill and co-operation of other road users to make filtering easier. Upset them and filtering riders may get hurt. The Highway Code and Motorcycle Roadcraft, in our opinion, do not offer much guidance to riders in how to do this legally and safely. Therefore, decision making is the responsibility of the individual, who will be responsible for their actions if it all goes wrong. Believe us, it does go wrong all too frequently. Where does this place you in the role of Trainer?

Any training input on filtering really does require the student to be proficient in balancing, steering and slow speed control. Check that they can do this first. How does a student become proficient in their filtering skills? The answer to that is to train using varying traffic conditions and situations. The more filtering is practiced, the easier it becomes and confidence increases. It is quite possible that a student starting these exercises still wobbles a little. This tendency will disappear quickly as the student becomes more familiar with what they need to do.

On your routes seek out where opportunities for filtering exist. Observe your student closely for hesitancy, as there will be times when they don't wish to go and yet "a bus could be driven through the gap". You may well see the student seeking sanctuary behind the vehicle in front, rather than positioned to its offside, to get a better view and to assess the gap correctly. Correct this and get the student to scan ahead, not just to look at what they want to avoid, which may well be the oncoming traffic. You appreciate the importance of scanning so reinforce this to your student. Yes, it is good for a student to be aware of vehicles in front and oncoming but get them to scan through the middle of the gap as far ahead as possible to better assess it, the hazards and if it is safe to go.

The approach to filtering successfully is to use **speed appropriate for the circumstances**. Do not let your student become influenced by what other riders do or become over confident. That will only end up in disaster. For example, when riding through a busy town, there is stop-start traffic in single file, both directions. We have seen it countless times, where riders will go down the offside of the queue too fast regardless of the hazards or the potential for things to happen to them. They do not appreciate the risks associated with their actions or behaviour. The road users being overtaken and the oncoming traffic, who may have to take avoiding action, will not appreciate it either. The riders may also show a total disregard for the law. It is not unusual for them to ride on the wrong side of lane separation bollards, go over give way and stop lines to get ahead of vehicles that are stationary and straddle junctions and clip door mirrors. And do not think this is just confined to passing four wheeled road users. There are riders out there that will jeopardise the safety of your students and you as well, by riding too fast, coming up on your near or off sides to get past, at ludicrous and unsafe speeds.

If the decision to filter down the offside of vehicles, as outlined above, is taken, then the sobering fact for your student to remember is that they will be riding on the wrong side of the road. If they are involved in a crash, then in all probability, they will be held to blame for it. It is very common for riders to be overtaking slow or stationary traffic on approach to a junction on the nearside and collide with a vehicle turning out of it. Do not let this happen to one of your students. Make sure they get their speed right. Generally, to ride past vehicles in this situation, your student should be riding between 2 to 8mph. There is a lot to observe and be aware of. A high level of anticipation is also needed and the ability to recognise a safe space to return to on their side of the road if circumstances make it necessary, for example, a bus is coming from the opposite direction, reducing the road width.

If the decision to filter down the nearside of traffic, as outlined in the above situation, is considered, your student must be aware of the added hazard of the kerb which restricts movement. The worst case scenario is to be sandwiched between a vehicle and the kerb. This must be avoided.

In multi-lane roads such as motorways, it is very common for all lanes to be one long traffic jam for miles. Clearly, the hard shoulder should not be used for filtering but there are riders that will do this. When filtering down the left or right of vehicles, remember that the principle is to use speed appropriate for the circumstances. A rider may also move from lane to lane because one lane stops and gaps appear left or right or a large truck narrows the space. Extra caution is needed when passing trucks as a rider will be in their blind spots. A rider does not want to be alongside a juggernaut when it suddenly moves lanes and space to escape is limited or non-existent.

Motorway speed limits are generally 70mph. Discuss with your student what the maximum speed of the traffic flow is for which they would consider filtering. You may be surprised by their response. Clearly at slow speeds and when it is safe to do so a rider can take advantage of filtering. So what is the cut off speed when a rider should adopt lane discipline and ride with the traffic flow? It certainly should be well below 70mph. What is practicable, reasonable and safe? Decisions, decisions, decisions... which your student and you will have to make.

In circumstances like this, as a guide, we use a passing speed of between 10 to 15 mph above the traffic flow, with the golden rule that if the gap narrows, reduce speed. Not many riders out there do this. So if the traffic is moving at 10mph consider filtering at 20 to 25mph.

A typical situation where filtering should be considered, is when local knowledge of a junction gives the opportunity to pass a queue of traffic. A junction your student is approaching is controlled by traffic lights. It has two lanes. The nearside is for turning left and going straight ahead and the offside is for turning right. The lights have just changed to red and traffic is stopping in the nearside lane. The offside lane is empty. Your student knows that when the traffic lights change to green, traffic in both lanes can enter the junction. By riding at a speed that is appropriate for the circumstances the student can ride in the offside lane to the stop line and be first away when the traffic lights go green. If the traffic lights change to red and amber or green on approach to the stop line the student can filter into the traffic on their left.

If the junction is controlled by a filter light for right turning traffic, then to occupy it waiting for the ahead light to illuminate would not be satisfactory, especially if vehicles behind were waiting to go. The student would not have thought this through properly and would be in the wrong lane in this situation. The golden rule in this case is, if any doubt about the layout of the junction and how the traffic signs operate, stay in the lane for the direction of travel intended.

OVERTAKING

Throughout your training delivery up to this point, you should have advised your students to "do what you would do normally" before overtaking. You will have sought not to influence their overtaking technique unless you felt the need to do so in reviewing a particular ride. A safe overtake necessitates a compromise between the speed of execution of the pass and the reduced following distance immediately prior to initiating the manoeuvre. The student needs to become comfortable with moving to a closer following distance and then, either executing the pass or dropping back again to the normal safe following distance.

Before commencing an overtaking training session, you will give a briefing, during which you will try to ascertain the students thinking processes. Most students will have been self-taught or had limited specific overtaking tuition. At the briefing you should stress that he should carry out his own ride and **must not** make any allowance for the presence of you, the Trainer. Any hesitation during an overtaking manoeuvre can literally be fatal and the Trainer will therefore only give information as to where he is on the road with respect to the student for example, "I am two vehicles behind, continue with your own ride until I catch up".

We should start with the scanning technique and the early recognition of a candidate vehicle on which an overtake manoeuvre can be executed. This will be the first occasion on which the slower moving vehicle is spotted, either as it emerged onto our road from a junction or as it appeared ahead of us.

What Information do we have? Are the weather, road and traffic conditions suitable? Are we likely to be able to execute a safe overtaking manoeuvre? Is the road surface suitable for fairly rapid acceleration; is the road wide and straight enough for a clear view of opposing traffic? Are there too many other hazards, such as junctions and bends? What about following traffic?

Only if these preconditions are satisfied would we consider moving from a normal following position (1) to the "formation" position (2) behind and to the offside of the vehicle.

The "formation" position (2) puts the rider in a more hazardous position than the normal following position (1) with less time and distance to react to changes, in speed or direction, of the vehicle to be overtaken.

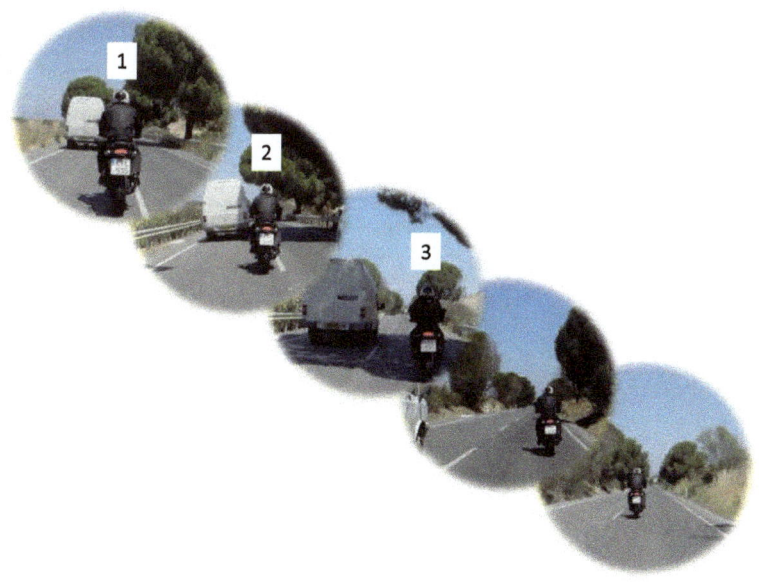

We move to this position (2) in order to reduce the time and distance spent on the wrong side of the road during the move to the "take-off" position (3) and the actual overtake. When we move to the "take-off" position (3) we will be in the best position to view the road and traffic ahead, prior to the final go or no go decision. Normally position 3 will be in the middle of the opposite carriageway on a two lane road to give sufficient margin of safety between the bike and the vehicle being overtaken. Your training to this point will have equipped the student to appreciate the power and gearing of his machine, in order to be able to accelerate smoothly but rapidly past the vehicle, if the Go decision is made. There must be no hesitation due to lack of familiarity with the motorcycle. We can use position number (1,2 and 3 above) as shorthand for speed of radio communication on the road.

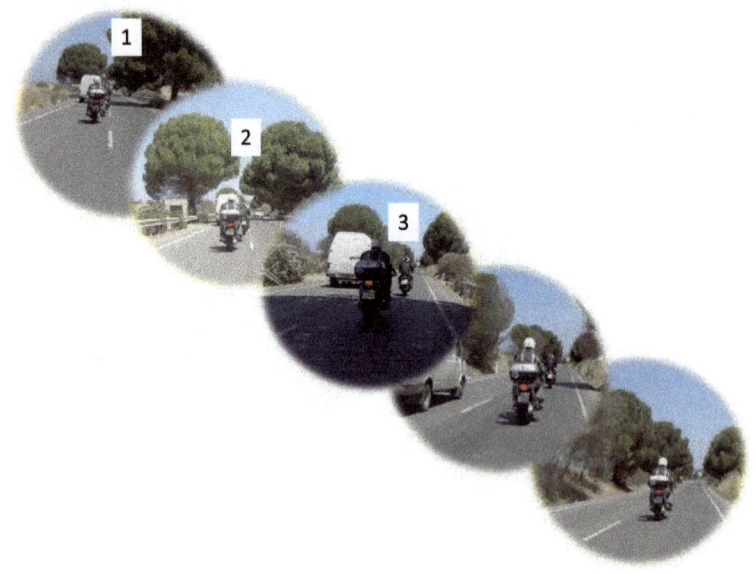

At the Go decision, all the work is done bar opening the throttle. IPSG is done and we have the final phase - Acceleration. The decision should be near instantaneous. If the student is in the take-off position (3) for more than a split second, they should have either gone or aborted and dropped back to position 2. Motto: If in doubt bottle out...and live to try again. Note that on moving from position 2 to 3 from "formation" to "take-off", most diagrams do not express what is to be done very well. It should be a gentle glide out to beyond the track of the vehicle to be overtaken. You want to maintain stability and have the bike in the most upright position for acceleration if the overtaking manoeuvre is on.

Likewise, being upright is most stable, if the decision is to brake/decelerate because, having recognised a hazard, the student needs to return to position 2 and then 1.

When should Lifesavers and signals be used? If you and your student are riding the road quickly and generally travelling faster than other vehicles, thereby giving rise to the opportunity and need for overtaking, what is behind you? Have your student's rearward observations been frequent and adequate to give confidence that no one is about to overtake? From the Trainer's perspective, if your student does a lifesaver before moving from position 2 to 3, you should find out why? Give feedback on the move about your observation but investigate the students thinking at debriefing, after the ride. It is most likely because his mirror checks were inadequate.

A lifesaver takes time, so, at speed, a rider needs to prioritise the vehicles and hazards ahead. At the same time he needs to be aware of those potentially approaching from the rear. On a single carriageway road, it will take up too much time and distance, forcing the rider to sacrifice forward, near distance, scanning and attention on behaviour of the vehicle in front. However, it is useful on a multi-lane, reasonably straight highway, both when moving out and when moving back. Other vehicles can approach quickly from behind and the forward vision does not have to take into account oncoming vehicles.

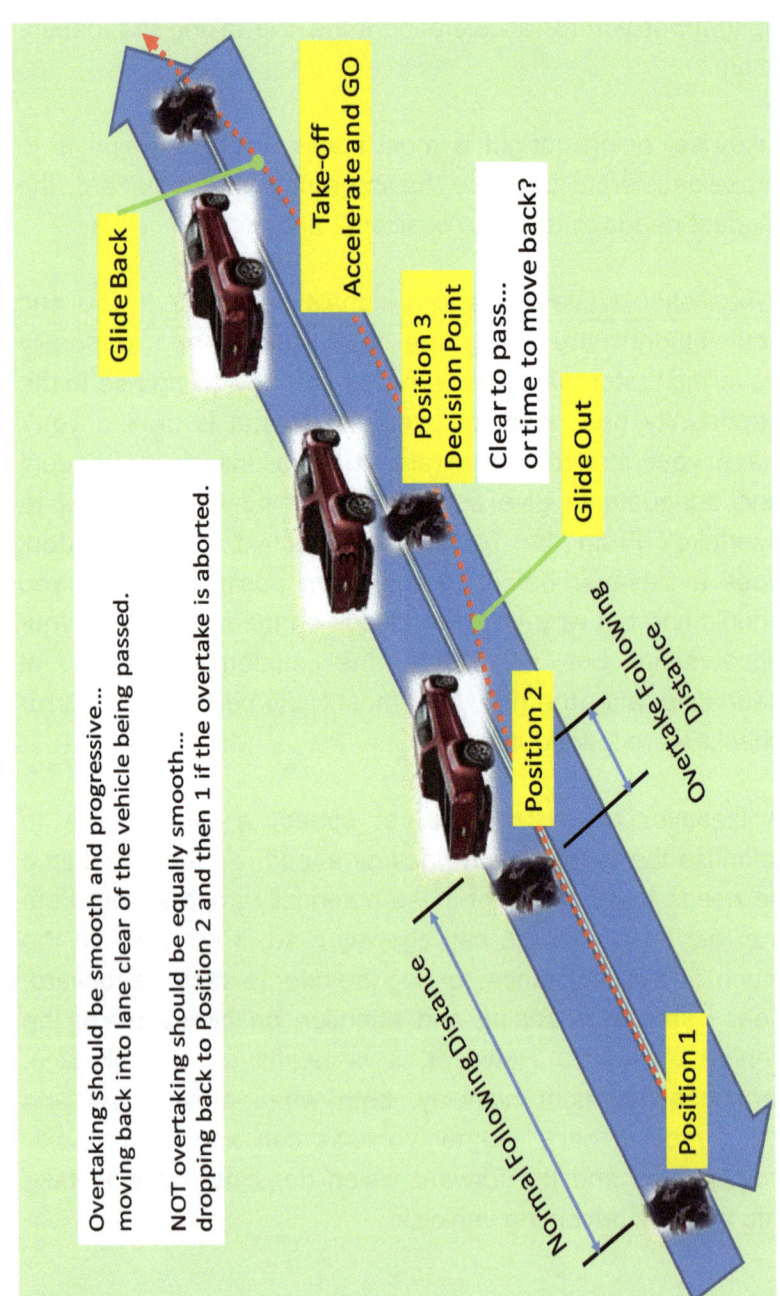

Overtaking should be smooth and progressive...
moving back into lane clear of the vehicle being passed.

NOT overtaking should be equally smooth...
dropping back to Position 2 and then 1 if the overtake is aborted.

Glide Back

Take-off
Accelerate and GO

Position 3
Decision Point

Clear to pass...
or time to move back?

Glide Out

Position 2

Overtake Following
Distance

Position 1

Normal Following Distance

On a highway there is never a need to move to position 2 and therefore, time to execute a lifesaver with each lane change.

Signalling is for the benefit of other road users. Who will benefit? If it provides reassurance to an oncoming vehicle that you are moving back to your side of the road: do one. Similarly if there is fast approaching traffic from the rear that can be advised of your intentions. Otherwise the birds do not need to know.

If you commence your overtake immediately after your student be aware that their overtake may be suddenly aborted for any reason and you will find yourself having to take avoiding action as they drop back.

Another common characteristic of students riding behaviour when overtaking is pass the vehicle(s) and then back off the gas, thereby reducing speed. Again you may have to take avoiding action. Ensure they maintain their speed or, if acceptable, increase it for their ride.

With knowledge of this type of behaviour it may be better for you to delay following them immediately in the early stages of their development until you have total confidence in their ability and both of you can overtake safely.

FINALLY...

So let us take the opportunity to remind you what being an Advanced Rider Trainer is all about:

Core competencies for you the Trainer
- understanding and knowledge of Motorcycle Roadcraft and The Highway Code
- qualified advanced rider and Trainer by certification
- ability to identify riding faults
- ability to analyse faults
- ability to remedy or rectify faults

Instructional techniques
- the appropriate level of training is matched to the ability of the student
- the planning of training sessions
- control of the training session
- communication skills
- question and answer techniques
- briefings, feedback and encouragement
- ensure briefings are a question and answer session – keep your student involved – they do have experience and a viewpoint
- always have your student give feedback to you to confirm that they fully understand what they will be doing before you ride
- and finally, remember to keep it simple

In Conclusion

Each student has different needs and abilities.

This handbook cannot deal with every eventuality that may arise or what you will experience when out with a student. That is where you own experiences, initiative and training skills come to the fore. If, like us, you continually say to yourself at the end of every ride

"What can I do to make it better?"

If you then act on your ideas, you will be a very successful Advanced Rider Trainer.

If there is something that you are unable to adapt to or need advice or guidance on, recognise this as an opportunity to expand your own knowledge and sound out what other professionals would do. If you are part of a voluntary organisation or road safety charity, generally there are senior Trainers or Examiners who are there to support you.

We wish you all the best on your future rides.

APPENDIX 1 – CHECKLIST FOR RIDERS

- ☐ eyesight test ☐ POWERED check
- ☐ visual examination / protective clothing
- ☐ attitude ☐ awareness
- ☐ anticipation ☐ IPSGA

Forward Observations

- ☐ scanning ☐ staring
- ☐ recognition of road signs
- ☐ two second rule
- ☐ hands follow eyes
- ☐ flexibility in riding seat ☐ obstructions
- ☐ available road width ☐ overtaking
- ☐ blind spots

Rearward Observations

- ☐ positioning of mirrors ☐ frequency of use
- ☐ used with IPSGA
- ☐ use of o/s mirror ☐ use of n/s mirror
- ☐ Lifesavers
- ☐ blind spots

Hand controls

- ☐ steering technique ☐ front brake
- ☐ clutch ☐ throttle
- ☐ use of indicators, timing and cancellation
- ☐ ancillary equipment

Foot controls

- ☐ gear lever ☐ rear brake

Riding skills

- ☐ positioning ☐ r/h bend
- ☐ l/h bend ☐ turn left ☐ turn right

- ☐ crossroads   ☐ crossroads with ATS
- ☐ roundabouts   ☐ zebra crossing
- ☐ pelican crossing ☐ single c/way
- ☐ dual c/way   ☐ motorway
- ☐ uphill start   ☐ downhill start
- ☐ angled start   ☐ use of ABS
- ☐ overtakes   ☐ vehicle sympathy
- ☐ acceleration sense   ☐ pillions
- ☐ hand signals   ☐ courtesy
- ☐ slow riding manoeuvres
- ☐ turn in the road ☐ use of side/main stand
- ☐ use of daytime headlight

APPENDIX 2 – PROGRESS TEMPLATE

Progress update – assessment ○ development ○
Name: Date: Trainer:
Vehicle details:

Attitude
Excellent ○ very good ○ good ○ average ○ poor ○
inconsistent ○
Comments:

Awareness
Excellent ○ very good ○ good ○ average ○ poor ○
inconsistent ○
Comments:

Anticipation
Excellent ○ very good ○ good ○ average ○ poor ○
inconsistent ○
Comments:

Observations
Excellent ○ very good ○ good ○ average ○ poor ○
inconsistent ○
Comments:

Practical skills
Excellent ○ very good ○ good ○ average ○ poor ○
inconsistent ○
Comments:

APPENDIX 3 - SCHEDULE OF SESSIONS

Session 1 – Assessment Ride

- POWERED checks
- Eyesight test
- Observation and scanning skill
- Machine control – use of brakes and gears, hands, feet and body positioning
- Hazard awareness
- Positioning
- Speed
- Attitude to other road users

Session 2 – IPSGA

- Explanation of what IPSGA means
- Discussion about use of signals
- Lifesavers
- Slow speed riding – figures of 8
- Use of front and rear brakes
- Back brake stops
- Left foot down

Session 3 – Bends

- Principle of limit points
- Walking the bends
- Control of speed based on limit point movement
- Sacrificing position for safety
- Straightlining
- Need for small amount of throttle

Session 4 - Town Work

- Hazards – fixed/moving/weather
- Speed and gears
- Filtering
- Rear brake/left foot down
- Positioning for junctions
- Taking advantage of street furniture
- Anticipation and being proactive as opposed to reactive

Session 5 – Roundabouts
- Scanning
- Lifesavers and mirror work
- Use of signals
- Speed matching
- Straightlining

Session 6 – Overtaking Part 1
- Scanning
- Lifesavers(when) and mirror work
- Planning
- Normal Following – Position 1
- Pre-overtake – Position 2
- "Take-off" Position 3
- Pull in
- Abort

Session 7 – Overtaking Part 2
- Recap Lesson 6
- Multi-lane riding

Session 8 through 10 – Perfecting
- Ask the student what he/she would like to revise
- Add your own recommendations from observations
- Less commentary as student perfects his/her technique
- Feedback is essential and should be regular and provide positive reinforcement if possible

About the Authors

Steve Tucker has been riding motor bikes for 40 years. As a UK Traffic Police Officer he was trained in advanced riding and driving skills. Riding a police motor bike in operational situations required a tremendous amount of expertise few riders can ever experience or achieve. Riding a motorbike for pleasure or commuting also requires an exceptional level of skill. Sadly, a large number of crash scenes he attended, where a biker was involved, were generally caused by rider error.

When he retired from the Police he used his knowledge and expertise of advanced riding and driving techniques to operate his own business in the UK Driver Training Industry. He was an Approved Driving Instructor, Grade 6 and a BTEC Progressive Advanced Driving Instructor at a time when the Industry was only just recognising the need to ensure Instructors were suitably qualified to provide expert training.

He now lives in Cyprus where the weather favours riders and provides them with mile after mile of great roads to ride. Riding motorbikes is a passion of Steve's and so is training. So it made a lot of sense to combine both passions and offer advanced rider training to the motorcyclists of Cyprus.

Steve is an Advanced Riding Tutor and an Advanced Riding Examiner for (Royal Society for the Prevention of Accidents (RoSPA) UK, and the training that he provides is based on Police Motor Cycle Roadcraft. Many riders including the Cyprus National Police and Sovereign Base Area Police Officers have benefited from advanced rider training with him. Advanced Rider Trainer is his first book on the subject.

David Rainford is an Advanced Motorcycle Rider with both the Institute of Advanced Motorists qualification and a RoSPA Gold Award. He is also a RoSPA qualified Advanced Rider Tutor.

Now living in Cyprus after a career in engineering design and consultancy, David has a degree in Aeronautical Engineering and a Diploma in Company Direction. He is a Chartered Mechanical Engineer and Commercial Drone Pilot.

However, first and foremost he is a real world biker, with a few lessons he learned the hard way. From falling off his first bike, a Honda C50 step-through, after an Emerson Lake & Palmer concert in 1971 to abusing a Ducati 900SS to cut a deer in half in 2000, David has realized that motorcycle safety comes from proper training and not just the experiences which did not kill or incapacitate the rider.

David brings to this book his knowledge of a systematic approach to engineering and management problem solving and considerable experience of staff appraisal, development and training.

Lightning Source UK Ltd.
Milton Keynes UK
UKHW020732200220
359042UK00005B/30

9 780957 452336